SAGE was founded in 1965 by Sara Miller McCune to support the dissemination of usable knowledge by publishing innovative and high-quality research and teaching content. Today, we publish over 900 journals, including those of more than 400 learned societies, more than 800 new books per year, and a growing range of library products including archives, data, case studies, reports, and video. SAGE remains majority-owned by our founder, and after Sara's lifetime will become owned by a charitable trust that secures our continued independence.

Los Angeles | London | New Delhi | Singapore | Washington DC | Melbourne

Advance Praise

This relatively slim volume written by a reputed economist presents a highly readable account of the explosion of demonetisation on the Indian economy, its wayward unfolding and unceremonious end; makes demonetisation a point of departure to suggest a comprehensive strategy for uprooting corruption; outlines a blueprint for the transition of India into a developed economy by 2050; and contains a succinct and penetrating review of four recent books on demonetisation—all in an easy-flowing and lucid style.

—Professor Muchkund Dubey
Chairman, Council for Social Development

There has been a wide-ranging debate on the effects of demonetisation of high-denomination notes. There was an overwhelming opinion of the economists and other knowledgeable persons suggesting that it failed to achieve the stated objectives, eroded credibility of some of our institutions, put the most vulnerable sections to great difficulty and, in any case, was grossly mismanaged. Dr Agarwala, while agreeing that there were some shortfalls, valiantly defends the government's basic position and points to what he regards as some unanticipated benefits coming from the move. For a healthy debate on such an important measure, it is necessary to hear the other side, and this is what Dr Agarwala's book offers.

Good, bad or indifferent, demonetisation has happened and cannot be reversed. We need to focus on where we go from here to achieve the central objective of reducing corruption in the country. This is where Dr Agarwala makes some bold suggestions which may be of interest to the public as well as the policy makers.

—Dr V.S. Vyas
Former Member, Economic Advisory Council to Prime Minister

DEMONETISATION

DEMONETISATION

A MEANS TO AN END?

RAMGOPAL AGARWALA

Los Angeles | London | New Delhi
Singapore | Washington DC | Melbourne

First published in 2017 by

 SAGE Publications India Pvt Ltd
B1/I-1 Mohan Cooperative Industrial Area
Mathura Road, New Delhi 110 044, India
www.sagepub.in

SAGE Publications Inc
2455 Teller Road
Thousand Oaks, California 91320, USA

SAGE Publications Ltd
1 Oliver's Yard, 55 City Road
London EC1Y 1SP, United Kingdom

SAGE Publications Asia-Pacific Pte Ltd
3 Church Street
#10-04 Samsung Hub
Singapore 049483

Published by Vivek Mehra for SAGE Publications India Pvt Ltd, typeset in 11/14 pts GillSans by Zaza Eunice, Hosur, Tamil Nadu, India and printed at Sai Print-o-Pack, New Delhi.

Library of Congress Cataloging-in-Publication Data

Names: Agarwala, Ramgopal, author.
Title: Demonetisation : a means to an end? / Ramgopal Agarwala.
Description: Thousand Oaks, California, USA : SAGE Publications, Inc., [2017]
  | Includes bibliographical references and index.
Identifiers: LCCN 2017026754| ISBN 9789386602138 (print pbk. : alk. paper) |
  ISBN 9789386602145 (e pub 2.0) | ISBN 9789386602152 (e book)
Subjects: LCSH: Monetary policy--India. | Corruption--Economic aspects--India.
Classification: LCC HG1235 .A66 2017 | DDC 332.4/954--dc23 LC record
available at https://lccn.loc.gov/2017026754

ISBN: 978-93-866-0213-8 (PB)

SAGE Team: Rajesh Dey, Guneet Kaur, Syeda Aina Rahat Ali and Rajinder Kaur

To all those who want to make
Bharat a global guru again

Thank you for choosing a SAGE product!
If you have any comment, observation or feedback,
I would like to personally hear from you.
Please write to me at **contactceo@sagepub.in**

Vivek Mehra, Managing Director and CEO, SAGE India.

Bulk Sales

SAGE India offers special discounts
for purchase of books in bulk.
We also make available special imprints
and excerpts from our books on demand.

For orders and enquiries, write to us at

Marketing Department
SAGE Publications India Pvt Ltd
B1/I-1, Mohan Cooperative Industrial Area
Mathura Road, Post Bag 7
New Delhi 110044, India

E-mail us at **marketing@sagepub.in**

Get to know more about SAGE

Be invited to SAGE events, get on our mailing list.
Write today to **marketing@sagepub.in**

This book is also available as an e-book.

Contents

ATM	Automatic Teller Machine
BJP	Bharatiya Janata Party
CNG	Compressed Natural Gas
CPI	Consumer Price Index
CRAR	Capital to Risk-weighted Assets Ratio
CRR	Cash Reserve Ratio
CSO	Central Statistical Organisation
DMS	Digital Monitoring System
DPS	Digital Payment System
EGC	Election Grants Commission
EU	European Union
FD	Fixed Deposit
FII	Foreign Institutional Investors
FRBM	Fiscal Responsibility and Budget Management
FTT	Financial Transaction Tax
GDP	Gross Domestic Product
GFCF	Gross Fixed Capital Formation
GOI	Government of India
G-secs	Government Securities
GST	Goods and Services Tax
HRD	Human Resource Development
ICS	Indian Civil Services
ICT	Information and Communication Technology
IFC	Indian Financial Code

List of Abbreviations

IIP	Index of Industrial Production
IT	Information Technology
LPG	Liquefied Petroleum Gas
MGNREGA	Mahatma Gandhi National Rural Employment Guarantee Act
MSME	Micro, Small and Medium Enterprises
MSP	Minimum Support Price
NII	Net Interest Income
NIPFP	National Institute of Public Finance and Policy
NPAs	Non-Performing Assets
OECD	Organisation for Economic Co-operation and Development
PBOC	People's Bank of China
POL	Petroleum, Oil and Lubricants
PSB	Public Sector Banks
RBI	Reserve Bank of India
SIT	Special Investigation Team
TBS	Twin Balance Sheet
UK	United Kingdom
UN	United Nations
USA	United States of America

Shyam Saran

Foreword

The sudden announcement of the demonetisation of high-value Indian currency notes of ₹1,000 and ₹500 on 8 November 2016 by the Prime Minister was an epoch-making but a controversial move generating sharply divergent opinions among both economists and politicians. Dr Ramgopal Agarwala, a highly respected economist and scholar, is eminently qualified to offer an informed and objective analysis of this decision and its consequences, both good and bad. He has argued that the key objective behind the demonetisation move was to root out corruption and the accumulation and circulation of illegally acquired wealth. While it did cause disruption in the economy and adversely affected the more vulnerable sections of society, it was lauded precisely by this same constituency largely because it was seen as a significant blow against endemic corruption. Furthermore, Dr Agarwala has argued that the informal sector, which economists and scholars said was worst affected by demonetisation, has proved to be far more resilient, and this is something which needs to be examined carefully. On balance, the economy has been put on a healthier trajectory, creating an environment for deep reform and higher growth. Dr Agarwala points out rightly that there is an imperative need to follow up with key reforms, which he has listed, including thorough reform of the taxation system, restructuring of the civil service and, above all, reform of funding of political parties. He argues that the public reaction to demonetisation demonstrates that the people of India are ready to support such reforms even if they entail some pain and dislocation in the near term.

I have worked with Dr Agarwala on a strategy of sustainable growth for India in the next several decades. He has written a celebrated book on the subject, containing a vision of a developed India in 2050. The strategy is based on the application of Gandhian values, such as the promotion of vegetarianism, which is resource frugal; the wider provision of public goods, such as efficient public transportation; and above all, the adoption of a new definition of affluence and good living, which is compatible with maintaining the fragile ecology of our planet. I consider this the most valuable insight which Dr Agarwala has put forward.

I compliment Dr Agarwala on his latest book and hope it will generate an informed debate on these larger issues, which is what we need at this time.

Shyam Saran
Former Foreign Secretary and Current Member,
Governing Board, Centre for Policy Research

At the midnight hour of 9 November 2016, two shock therapies were being administered on two sides of the globe, the United States of America (USA) and India. In the USA, against all the forecasts of election pundits and my fellow economists, Donald Trump was winning in one constituency after another. In India, Prime Minister Modi had announced that after the midnight of 8 November, Indian notes of ₹500 and ₹1,000 would cease to be legal tender except for some specified uses, and the holders had until December 30 to deposit their notes in the banks for conversion into new notes. Pandemonium broke out in India, and people were flocking to shops (particularly jewellery shops) to use their notes to purchase whatever they could before midnight. An avalanche of criticism was coming on television and local newspapers.

In his announcement, the Prime Minister mentioned the rationale for his action and the exceptions that were being put in to minimise the pain to the public. He said:

> It has been a matter of concern for all of us that corruption and black money tend to be accepted as part of life. This type of thinking has afflicted our politics, our administration and our society like an infestation of termites. None of our public institutions is free from these termites…

Preface

To break the grip of corruption and black money, we have decided that the ₹500 and ₹1,000 currency notes presently in use will no longer be legal tender from midnight tonight, that is, 8 November 2016. This means that these notes will not be acceptable for transactions from midnight onwards. The ₹500 and ₹1,000 notes hoarded by anti-national and anti-social elements will become just worthless pieces of paper. The rights and the interests of honest, hard-working people will be fully protected. Let me assure you that notes of ₹100, ₹50, ₹20, ₹10, ₹5, ₹2 and ₹1 and all coins will remain legal tender and will not be affected.

To minimise the difficulties of citizens in the coming days, several steps were announced. Persons holding old notes of ₹500 or ₹1,000 could deposit these notes, without any limit, in their bank or post office accounts from 10 November until the close of banking hours on 30 December 2016. They could also exchange the old notes for new ones up to a limit. Also, for 72 hours, old notes were accepted at pharmacies in government hospitals; railway ticket booking counters; ticket counters of government buses; airline ticket counters at airports; petrol, diesel and compressed natural gas (CNG) stations authorised by public sector oil companies; consumer cooperative stores authorised by state or central government; milk booths authorised by state governments; and crematoria and burial grounds.

The Prime Minister mentioned four objectives of his initiative. The first and foremost was to curb corruption. This was connected with unearthing of 'black money' which was generated by income that had not been declared to tax authorities. It was also aimed at foiling currency counterfeiting and curbing terrorist activities, which use high-denomination notes. This was not an isolated stand-alone step but part of a package of activities aimed at checking black money, which were started soon after the new government came to power. In 2014 itself, it was announced that a special investigation team (SIT) would be formed to investigate the modalities for bringing back black money stashed abroad. This was followed by the Black Money and Imposition of Tax Act, 2015 and Benami Transactions (Prohibition) Amended Act, 2016. There was an information exchange agreement with Switzerland; moreover, tax treaties which might have been facilitating black money transactions were revised for Mauritius, Cyprus and Singapore. Income declaration scheme was announced, giving an option to erstwhile tax evaders to come clean with modest penalties, and these were accompanied by stern warnings from the Prime Minister himself that those who did not come forward will face harsh consequences.

The announcement of 8 November had, I thought, noble objectives, and something good was happening in India. However, I was surprised how virulent were the criticisms of demonetisation by most of my economist friends in India and the USA. I was also impressed by stories of how the common man was welcoming the demonetisation initiative in spite of the temporary hardships. The hypothesis I thought worth exploring was that the elites in India and their counterparts abroad were just out of touch with the masses who had an utter disgust with all-pervading corruption in India and saw demonetisation as a way of doing something about it.

I read with interest Pankaj Mishra's book *Age of Anger: A History of the Present* (2017). Mishra notes that in the mid-19th century Europe, there were young provincials (like Rousseau) who 'simmered with resentment against a largely metropolitan civilization of slick movers and shakers that seemed to deny them a rooted and authentic existence'. He goes on to argue that there may be a similar resentment in the West at present. The rise of Trump may indicate the surge of resentment of the common man in the USA against the elites.

Perhaps in India too, the rise of Modi and more recently of Yogi Adityanath indicate a surfacing of a similar resentment and revolt of the masses against the Westernised elites. There may also be some truth in the argument that in India, for many decades, the masses had accepted the Westernised elites as natural rulers following the British rule, but that phase is ending. It may be worthwhile to look at the demonetisation episode in the context of this battle between the Westernised elites and masses for understanding and managing India with respect to the problem of all-pervading corruption.

Over the years, corruption has been spreading like a cancer through the body politic of India. There is a deeply felt public disgust with the situation, and any leader seen as fighting against the disease inspires widespread following, as was the case with Anna Hazare's movement against corruption in 2010. However, over the years, the problem has been getting worse, not better. This might be at least in part due to a flawed understanding on the part of the Westernised elites of the problem of corruption in India. It was seen mainly as a public sector governance problem. But it was not realised that public sector corruption was possible only because there was a large private sector, willing and able to fund that corruption. In fact, the business world was the fountainhead of corruption, and black money was the main poison that flew from that fountain. Prime Minister Modi, with his instinctive understanding of the business world and the problem of corruption, zeroed in on black money as the key problem of corruption and set in motion a programme to disrupt the fountainhead that produced the poison. He announced a demonetisation programme which was intended to punish the holders of black cash and bring all money held in that world into the open in the banking channels.

The Westernised elites who have been ruling India since Independence saw this as an opportunity to malign the desi Prime

Minister and weaken his political base. They, with the Left and the Right combining in this endeavour, unleashed a virulent volley of criticisms of the most extreme type. Fortunately, the adverse effects of demonetisation were not as serious as the Westernised elites made it out to be, and the masses took the hardships in their stride.

Unfortunately, most of the black money holders found ways of laundering their black money, and the gains from demonetisation fell short of expectations.

At the same time, the exercise had some unanticipated benefits in the form of strengthening the hands of the political leaders to carry on their struggle for a corruption-*mukt* (corruption-free) Bharat. Corruption, it was realised, is like blood cancer; it needs a long-term treatment and not just a surgical strike. The electorate seemed inclined to give the political leaders the time necessary to achieve that objective.

Demonetisation in India, thus, was not a financial exercise. It was about curing corruption and achieving clean growth. The electorate has strengthened the hands of the government to strive for not only cleaner India but also richer India. The Prime Minister has articulated his long-term vision of India.

> I believe India is standing at a watershed moment, on the cusp of actualizing its inherent potential as a developed nation and global leader. An India that is Swachh from all forms of filth.... I am... putting my heart and soul into building an enabling environment to spark a revolution that transforms India into a developed nation within one generation. I am confident the country can, and will.

If India can indeed become a developed nation within a generation, it will reclaim its position as the largest economy in the world, a position it occupied for nearly 1,000 years around the beginning of the first millennium. In that position, it can also become a beacon (a guru) for the world for realizing a clean, democratic and ecologically healthy society.

The two shocks of 9 November 2016 may thus be connected not only by the revolt of the masses against the elites but also through the changing roles of the USA and India in world affairs. Through the shock of electing Donald Trump, the USA, on the one hand, was initiating a process (perhaps a long one) of withdrawing from the leadership role of the democratic world that it assumed after the Second World War. India, on the other hand, with its demonetisation announcement initiated a process (also a long one) of a cleaner India leading to a prosperous India capable of becoming a global guru for democratic, spiritually oriented and ecologically sustainable prosperity.

If India is to fulfil its potential as suggested by the twin shocks of 9 November 2016, a lot of hard work lies ahead to clear the misunderstandings about what is going on in India in the context of demonetisation, and to chart and travel the path to its destiny. In this book, we offer our humble suggestions in both these areas.

At my age of 79, agreeing to write a book on the hot and complex topic of demonetisation within two months was a bold decision. I could not have taken that without powerful persuasion from Rajesh Dey, Commissioning Editor at SAGE, and my wife Bimala. However, I was started on the track by my friend Anand Gupta who asked me to give a talk on demonetisation to the Rotary Club of South Delhi. While preparing for the talk, I started reflecting on the subject, and I began to feel that my Marwari background gave me a unique insight into the world of black money, which my fellow economists and bureaucrats with Anglicised backgrounds did not have. I thought that I need to tell the story from the perspective my background has afforded.

As I started to write the draft, I got some extraordinary help from Rajesh Dey. I spent 50 years of my professional life first in number crunching as an econometrician and then as a policy analyst at the World Bank. My favourite tools were numbers and bullet points. And in the World Bank style, I was accustomed to summarise my conclusions and policy proposals right at the beginning to help the reader evaluate my conclusions. But Rajesh told me that this book is meant for the general reader and should be in a different style. Instead of stating my conclusions at the very beginning, I should take the readers on a journey, at the end of which they will arrive at their own conclusions. And through the entire journey, I would have to hold their interest!! It was quite an exercise to change my lifelong habits. But I saw the logic of the points and

Acknowledgements

worked assiduously with Rajesh to discard my favourite tools and make the transformation.

Rajesh proved to be a tough taskmaster while performing the delicate task of guiding an old professor continuously. We both worked hard at this book, and it is for the reader to decide how far we have succeeded. I am deeply grateful to Rajesh for his help and would like to put on record my appreciation of his great editorial abilities. I am most grateful to the editorial team of SAGE which included Guneet Kaur Gulati and Syeda Aina Rahat Ali.

At the World Bank, while working on a project like this, I would have a whole team of colleagues to help me do research and act as a sounding board for my arguments. Pahle India Foundation is a small organisation with only limited resources. But I was lucky to get excellent research assistance from Dnyanada Palkar who, despite all her other duties, provided me with data and material as and when I needed them.

For the last two months, I have felt like a college student Googling like mad and also searching through libraries for books and magazines. In this effort, I got wonderful support from the library staff of three excellent libraries: Lok Sabha Library, Nehru Memorial Library and the library at the India Habitat Centre. The Director of Nehru Memorial Library, Shakti Sinha, was kind enough to organise a seminar on my draft, which acted as a peer review process for me and helped me to improve the draft. During the seminar and also later, I got valuable feedback from Subhomoy Bhattacharjee, John Elliot, Anand Gupta, Rajiv Kumar, Anupam Khanna, Ravi Mishra and Nirupama Soundararajan.

Among the others from whom I had the benefit of feedback were Shankar Acharya, Anil Sood, Mark Tully, my son-in-law Carsten Stendedvad, and above all my wife, who was experiencing the real-life drama of demonetisation and had many good pieces of advice all along.

I am grateful to Ambassador Shyam Saran for writing the Foreword for this book. It brings out beautifully the key features of the book, particularly the reforms we need in order to achieve a clean and prosperous India.

Anil Kumar Gupta of Pahle India Foundation provided admirable support in formatting my draft and doing everything I needed in the world of the Internet.

Taking advantage of my age and absence of bureaucratic constraints, I was inclined to speak my mind without fear or favour and was running the risk of going too far out on sensitive matters and even offending my fellow economists. I got immense help in self-restraint from my family and friends, particularly my wife Bimala, my son-in-law Carsten and Mark Tully. I still remain outspoken, and I hope the reader will take my strong opinions as expressions of my passion to serve my motherland and forgive me for my excesses.

Public Revulsion against Corruption in India

In India, corruption is like a termite that is eating away its body and soul. The public is looking for leaders who can do something about it.

Corruption as Cancer of the Indian Society

The demonetisation exercise is, on the face of it, a financial affair. Generally, it is undertaken in the context of excessive money supply causing hyperinflation and instability in the economy. But in India, there was no such emergency and no need to demonetise for financial reasons. Indian demonetisation was a different creature altogether. The exercise was basically propelled, as the Prime Minister said in his announcement, by the desire to check corruption and build the foundations for clean prosperity. Thus, to understand the developments in India following demonetisation and public's reaction to the exercise, we need to understand the issue of corruption in India and how it hurts the programme for prosperity for all. And I begin with some personal experience in this regard.

In 2005, after 40 years of living abroad in England, Canada and the USA, I returned to my motherland. During this period, I had had the good fortune of studying at close quarters some 20 countries, both developed and developing, around the world with my last assignment being as chief economist of the World Bank in

Beijing, China. On the basis of my experience, I concluded that as individuals Indians are just as capable as anybody in the world, and there is no inherent reason why India should not become a developed country. The Indian economy was growing at more than 8 per cent per year, and the vision of India becoming a developed country with prosperity of all seemed eminently credible. However, corruption was spreading as a termite and becoming a way of life. That, I thought, would never allow India to achieve efficiency necessary for sustained growth.

At a personal level, it was painful to find that it was difficult, if not impossible, to live honestly in India. Whether I was dealing with public sector agencies or the private sector, it was impossible to go around without resorting to bribes or use of black money. It was also striking that the informal sector, where cash was the king and labour laws were ignored, was a dominant part of the economy. Over the years, I noted the growing incidence of corruption and increasing share of black money, which was also driving asset prices (particularly land and housing) to totally unreal levels. When I wanted to buy a residence, I found that the price of an apartment in Delhi was higher than its comparator in Washington, DC. Over the years, I found it sickening to observe the flamboyant lifestyle of the newly rich with wads of currency notes thrown around in their shopping spree. My heart cried to see Gandhi's India, about whose spiritual capital I had been singing in my 40 years in the West, reeking in corruption all around me. I cried, saying, *meri Ganga maili ho gayee* (My revered Ganga has gone dirty).

Some economists argue that corruption is the lubricant that helps move the wheels of a controlled economy and is often associated with economic progress. Bollywood movies have articulated well how rise of some industrial magnets in India was facilitated by corruption in high places. History of industrialised countries such as the UK and the USA is also replete with examples of how industrial magnets manipulated political systems to gain special advantages. In East Asian countries such as Japan, South Korea and China too, corruption was a big part of their economic rise.

However, in India, corruption, particularly the one associated with black money, has been highly detrimental to growth. Let us note three areas where black money contributes to poor investment and loss of growth. Black money is hot money looking for quick movement. One such area for quick absorption of black money has been the buying of land, and that process has pushed land prices to extremely high levels, yielding unearned income or 'rent' to holders of land. Money which in white form could have gone to investment in factories or social and physical infrastructure goes into unproductive investment in land, thus costing the country much-needed growth. Another pernicious form of the use of black money is in dowry and expensive wedding which apart from being a missed opportunity for investment is a most obnoxious social phenomenon with terrible effect on the position of girls in the family. The situation has become so bad that in the recent general elections, there were cases where the contestants when asked to report their assets and liabilities listed daughters as liability! A third form of distortion is black money going abroad through hawala channels and through a peculiarly Indian institution of participatory notes coming back to the Indian stock market and adding instability to the market. Under this system, Indians can buy from foreign investment bankers the participatory notes for dollars with no questions asked, and they can then invest these funds in the Indian stock market in white.

In India, we often look to the Anglo-American world as our role model. But corruption remains a big problem in these countries, and they cannot be our role models if we want a clean India. Better role models are available in Northern European countries such as Norway, Sweden, Denmark, Finland, Germany and the Netherlands. These countries have managed to keep corruption levels low as shown by reports of Transparency

International. They have a high degree of tax compliance and have been able to use tax revenues to provide health, education and social security benefits to the masses. Contrary to the theories in the Anglo-American world, high taxation has not led to loss of economic efficiency and vibrancy. These countries have been able to combine prosperity for all, with equity and transparency leading to high levels in the happiness index. If we want a clean India with *sabka saath sabka vikas* (collective efforts, inclusive growth), we should turn our gaze away from the Anglo-American world towards these Northern European countries.

Equally important as the economic argument is the moral argument. Honesty is the basic ingredient of a healthy mental and spiritual life. India, a land of deep spiritual traditions, can never accept corruption as a way of life. The Indian soul was crying as corruption was spreading.

India's Losing Battle against Corruption

Guided by these fundamental truths, Indian public never accepted the facile argument that corruption is necessary for prosperity. Various anti-corruption measures were taken regularly after Independence. Among the efforts to combat corruption in the public sector in recent years, two important measures were The Prevention of Corruption Act, 1988 and The Right to Information Act, 2005. The former widened the scope of the definition of a 'public servant', enhanced penalties provided for offences in earlier laws, incorporated the provisions of freezing of suspected property during trial, mandated trial on a day-to-day basis and prohibited the grant of stay on trial. The Right to Information Act, 2005, under which any person can seek any information from the concerned public authority just by filing an application at almost no cost, is regarded as a revolutionary measure. The public authority has to reply to the application compulsorily within 30 days. India has also been cooperating with United Nations (UN) agencies on various initiatives for checking corruption.

But the incidence of corruption continued to increase instead of decreasing. Was there some basic flaw in the diagnosis and/or prescription of the anti-corruption movements? Are there better and newer ways to check corruption, particularly with the advent of information technology? Let us briefly review the sad history of trying to move towards a corruption-*mukt* Bharat.

In pre-Independence days, Mahatma Gandhi got an inkling of the corrupting potential of power, when in 1937 the Indian National Congress formed ministries in six provinces under the 1935 Act. Charges of corruption against ministers and legislators began to fly thick and fast. Mahatma was perturbed and wrote, 'I would go the length of giving the whole Congress a decent burial, rather than put up with corruption that is rampant'. But Congress was not buried, and corruption only got worse during World War II that came soon.

During the war, there were acute scarcities of many essential goods. Owing to the criminal neglect of the British government and the callousness of Sir Winston Churchill, Bengal was thrown into a disastrous famine. Hoarding and black marketing became widespread, and I can remember stories of businessmen practising hoarding and angry public surrounding businessmen's godowns with relief provided by police on payment for their help.

Scarcities continued in the post-war era, with partition adding fuel to the fire, particularly in eastern India. Corruption was rampant. Nehru thundered, 'In free India, corrupt and black marketers will be hanged from the nearest lamp post'. With freedom at midnight, scarcities were greater than ever and so was corruption. Not much hanging took place, and Nehru's remark remained only as a reminder of the seriousness of the problem of corruption and poor capacity of the government to tackle it.

With improved supply of essential goods, rationing was being slowly relaxed in the 1950s, and the incidence of corruption relating to distribution of essential goods was coming down. But a new source of corruption was emerging. Nehru was under the spell of what may be called the 'Moscow Consensus' of central planning. Nehru had written eloquently on how the Soviets made great progress in industrialisation through planning under Stalin and how that industrialisation and planning helped the Soviet Union to fight and defeat Hitler's forces. Under the planning mode, the total resources of the country were assumed to be fixed (without taking into account simulative effects on productivity that can flow from the right system of incentives and distribution). The state had to own the commanding heights of the economy and allocate resources for the public as well as the private sector. The private sector cannot be allowed to invest and produce according to market forces. This led to what has been aptly termed the licence–permit–quota raj. It is the bureaucrats who would decide what the private sector can invest and produce. But the private sector in India was large and powerful and the bureaucratic capacities limited. Contrary to the popular narrative, the private sector did quite well under the regime of licences, permits and quotas with a lot of windfalls from these restrictions which could be relaxed with suitable payment to the bureaucrats for their services. Despite Nehru's clean heart and disdain for the business world, corrupt businessmen along with corrupt bureaucrats and politicians were shining under the lamp posts rather than being hanged from there. There was a clear mismatch between Nehru's economic policy and aspirations for a clean India.

With growing corruption, there was clamour for action. In 1962, Home Minister Lal Bahadur Shastri, who had a strong ethical mooring, succeeded in persuading Prime Minister Nehru to appoint a high-power committee under the chairmanship of Shri K. Santhanam (MP) to examine the problem of corruption and come up with remedies. The committee was primarily focused on central services of the Government of India (GOI), though it was mentioned that the committee could also look at broader dimensions of the problem.

The committee report did not do much more than making the usual noises about the reform of civil service procedures. Despite the lukewarm recommendations, the committee report could have been a catalyst for reforms with personal interest in the cleaner India of Lal Bahadur Shastri, who was soon to become the prime minister. But with the untimely death of Shastri, the missionary for ethics was gone, and soon a different atmosphere prevailed.

Corruption began to be ingrained in India's polity with Indira Gandhi's rise to power. When asked about corruption, she shot back, 'Corruption is a global phenomenon'. Without an ethical centre of gravity of the freedom fighters and faced with a struggle for power within the Congress party, she let loose the virus of corruption in the Indian polity. Under the rhetoric of poverty removal, she tightened the licence–permit–quota raj, thereby increasing the power of her regime to collect 'rent' from the business world which she could distribute to her supporters. As narrated by S.S. Gill (1998, 69),

> L.N. Mishra, who was appointed independent minister of state for commerce, made full use of the 'license–quota–permit raj' and attached price-tag to every license, permit or clearance he issued. He collected huge amounts of money, and disbursed it like a king. As a matter of routine sealed envelopes were dispatched from his house to a variety of beneficiaries who included not only politicians, but also journalists and all sorts of touts. Of course, Mishra was only a puppet and the strings were pulled by the master strategist.

The venom ran through the system with increasing sway even when regimes changed. Even Dr Manmohan Singh, an eminent man with unimpeachable credentials, allowed corruption under the name of coalition dharma. The Great Liberalization, which he was forced by circumstances to introduce in 1991 and which was supposed to reduce corruption, was of no great help, and corruption was greater in 2010 than in 1990.

Over the years, major scandals were emerging in the states and at the Centre and in various sectors covering media, films, educational institutions, medical institutions, financial institutions, big businesses as well as not-so-big businesses, and domestic suppliers as well as foreign suppliers.

The farce and tragedy of corruption in India were dramatised in 2010 by Niira Radia tapes. The tapes revealed that the lobbyist working for powerful corporate houses was in telephone conversations with political leaders, corporate honchos and media icons and was able to play a role in the formation of the Central Cabinet to cater to the wishes of corporate world. Moreover, she was able to persuade leading television anchors and leading figures in print media to give spin to news reports and analyses to suit the purposes of her clients. There was shame and embarrassment all round.

Public disgust with corruption was becoming loud and clear. It crystallised in the support extended to Anna Hazare, a social activist who on 5 April 2011 started a 'fast unto death' to exert pressure on the government to enact a strong anti-corruption act to establish a Lokpal (ombudsman) with the power to deal with corruption in public life. The movement was in Gandhian tradition, featuring demonstrations, hunger strikes, marches and rallies, as well as the use of social media to organise, communicate and raise awareness.

Anna Hazare's demand was narrowly based on creating a legal framework and not any other specific policy reform. The government, which did not have its heart in anti-corruption measures, found it easy to diffuse the movement by agreeing to Hazare's demand and forming a joint committee which included civil society representatives to draft legislation on Lokpal. Even though framed in the Gandhian mode, the whole movement of Anna Hazare lacked deep understanding of the problem and the Gandhian capacity for strategic focus. It soon fizzled out. But the interesting thing was the support extended by the public. The movement attracted thousands of supporters. Hundreds joined him in his fast. The youth expressed its massive support on social media sites. Protests in support of Anna occurred in many cities, including Bengaluru, Mumbai, Chennai, Ahmedabad, Guwahati and Aizawl. Clearly, the country wanted a cleaner India. I could hear the echo of my cry: *meri Ganga maili ho gayee hai.* The elite just did not connect with the disgust that the common man felt about corruption. The standard social scientists (particularly economists) try to be value-free as scientists are supposed to be. To them, the words morality and spirituality are anathema. But to the common man, these are foundational values. They want a value-based polity. The fact that even Anna Hazare without any clear programme could attract so much public support showed how disgusted the public is with corruption and how ready it is to extend support to a leader who promises to do something about it. It is in such an atmosphere that demonetisation came.

Black Money: A Key Facilitator of Corruption

Chapter 2

Contrary to the conventional wisdom, business world is the
fountain-head of black money which spreads corruption
throughout the system and black money phenomenon cannot
be understood by economists working with white data.

Business World as Fountain Head of Corruption and Black Money

The tragic failure of India in combating corruption calls for deep reflections. Lack of political will, lack of political power, old colonial era rules of governance, old traditions of satiating power through gifts, excessive levels of taxation and regulatory system—all these played important roles in perpetuating corruption. But in our opinion, there were some fundamental flaws in the government's approach. First, there was too much of focus on government as the source of corruption and a failure to understand the wider societal sources of poison that feeds corruption. Second, there was too much reliance on academic economic research with little familiarity with the real Indian conditions.

Following the triumph of the theory of 'magic of market place' popularised in the Anglo-American world by Margaret Thatcher and Ronald Reagan, it has become customary to blame all maladies of the country on the state and present the business world as an angel trying to take the country to new heights of prosperity and progress. Since the reform of 1991, India is still under the spell of Thatcher–Reagan revolution, although in the UK and the USA many dissenting voices are being raised. However, it is worth recalling what the Santhanam Committee said in 1962 about the role of private sector in generating corruption.

The Santhanam Committee noted:

> Corruption can exist only if there is someone willing to corrupt and capable of corrupting. We regret to say that both this willingness and capacity to corrupt is found in a large measure in the industrial and commercial classes. It is these persons who indulge in evasion and avoidance of taxes, accumulate large amounts of output through without accounting for it in bills and accounts (on-money) and under-valuation of transactions in immovable property. It is they who have control over large funds and are in a position to spend considerable sums of money in entertainment. It is they who maintain an army of liaison men and contact men, some of whom live, spend and entertain ostentatiously…. Contractors and suppliers who have perfected the art of getting business by under-cutting, of making good the loss by passing off sub-standard works and goods generally spare no pains or expenditure in creating a favorable atmosphere. *Possession of large amounts of unaccounted money by various persons including those belonging to the industrial and commercial classes is a major impediment in the purification of public life.* (Emphasis added)

The message of the Santhanam Committee has much relevance today and the business world is probably the fountain head of corruption and poison of black money. Coming from a business community I have seen from my childhood how black money was created in businesses. The money that flows from that fountain is the biggest source of corruption in the society. This flow in the business world is much bigger than the flow of corrupt money in the public sector. The deleterious effects of black money are found in some major distortions in the economy connected with real estate, gold and jewellery, conspicuous consumption including ostentatious weddings, and leakage of capital abroad.

The size and power of the black economy can be guessed from what has been happening in some key sectors which are closely connected with black money. Anybody familiar with the insides of the black economy knows that black money is hot money looking for quick transmission. I can recall personal episodes where a substantial amount of money was generated in black and that had to go into real estate as safer forms of storage, irrespective of what it does in driving up the prices of land and housing. This has led to bubble in the prices of these assets much beyond the buying capacity of the honest public and much above the prices in comparator countries. The hot money also flows relentlessly into gold and jewellery, causing surge in imports much beyond what was customary. And then there are ever-increasing hawala transactions, where the owners of black money try to salt their money away from the gaze of the country's tax authorities to foreign lands.

Pseudo-scientific Efforts to Estimate Black Economy from White Data

Over the years, many attempts have been made to estimate black economy and black money in India and elsewhere. There is no universally accepted definition of black money. Generally, it is defined to cover the part of the economy that operates legally but remains outside the ken of the authorities to avoid taxation and other regulations. There is of course the additional sphere of economic activities which indulge in illegal operations such as smuggling, drug dealing and human trafficking and are also outside the ken of official agencies. The second category is hard to estimate and is generally kept out of estimates of black economy.

In India, one of the earliest estimates was made by Professor Nicholas Kaldor of Cambridge University in connection with his report on taxation in India. He estimated non-salary income on the basis of the break-up of national income into

1. Wages and salaries,

2. Income of the self-employed and

3. Profit, interest, rent, etc.

Excluding wages and salaries from the contribution to net domestic product, he derived total non-salary income. *An estimate of the actual non-salary income assessed to tax was made for each sector* in order to arrive at the total non-salary income assessed to tax. The difference between *the estimated non-salary income above the exemption limit* and the actual non-salary income assessed to tax measures the size of 'black' income.

It was not clarified how the estimates of actual non-salary income assessed to tax were made in each sector and how the exemption limit for the sector (which is quite different from an individual's exemption limit) was calculated.

A well-known study on black economy in India was done in 1985 by National Institute of Public Finance and Policy (NIPFP) under the guidance of Dr Shankar Acharya. To prepare a global estimate of black income, the NIPFP study confined itself to six areas:

1. Factor incomes received either openly or covertly while participating in the production of goods and services,

2. 'Black' income generated in relation to capital receipts on sale of asset,

3. 'Black' income generated in fixed capital formation in the public sector,

4. 'Black' income generated in relation to the private corporate sector,

5. 'Black' income generated in relation to export and

6. 'Black' income generated through over invoicing of imports by the private sector and sale of import licences.

There was no clarification on how these estimates of black income in different sectors were made. There were probably just guess estimates by economists with little knowledge of the black economy in any of these sectors.

In 2010, the World Bank published a study on black economy authored by Friedrich Schneider, Andreas Buehn and Claudia E. Montenegro. It used the term shadow economy instead of black economy but its definition was basically the same which included all market-based legal production of goods and services that are deliberately concealed from public authorities to avoid payment of income, value added or other taxes, to avoid payment of social security contributions, having to meet certain legal labour market standards such as minimum wages, maximum working hours and complying with certain administrative procedures.

The authors recognised that it is very difficult to get accurate information about shadow economy activities, including the goods and labour involved, because individuals engaged in these activities do not wish to be identified. But they hoped to have some magic tricks of statistics by which they will estimate the extent of shadow economy without any concrete numbers of them.

While several researchers may be struggling for years to estimate the size of shadow economy for a single country and a single year, the authors declared with due immodesty that their goals were '(i) to undertake the challenging task of estimating the shadow economy for 162 countries in various stages of development and located in several regions throughout the world and (ii) to provide some insights about the main causes of the shadow economy'.

In the absence of data on shadow economy, the authors looked for *some general comparable proxies*. In the good old tradition of the World Bank blaming everything including existence of shadow economy on government interference, the authors used the following causal variables: (a) Share of direct taxes—direct taxes as a proportion of overall taxation (positive sign expected), (b) Size of government—general government final consumption expenditures (per cent of gross domestic product [GDP], which includes all government current expenditures for purchases of goods and services; positive sign expected) and (c) Fiscal freedom—a subcomponent of the Heritage Foundation's Index of Economic Freedom, which measures the fiscal burden in an economy, that is, top tax rates on individual and corporate incomes. The index ranges from 0 to 100, where 0 is least degree of fiscal freedom and 100 is maximum degree of fiscal freedom (negative sign expected).

The authors went on to describe their complicated methodology by which these variables were presumed to determine the size of the shadow economy and then used their estimated equation from global experience to deduce the size of shadow economy in individual countries over time.

Using their pseudo-sophisticated techniques, the authors claimed to determine the share of shadow economy in all countries with widely varying economic conditions by macroeconomic variables such as size of government, share of direct taxation, fiscal freedom, business freedom, unemployment rate, GDP per capita and government effectiveness.

Their approach was presumed to apply to India as to China or Singapore with the specificities of these countries totally ignored. In the Indian context, agricultural income is not subject to income tax and one would expect that the share of agricultural income would have some bearing on the share of shadow economy. Similarly, GDP generated in public sector should not have a shadow income component and thus the share that public sector forms of the economy should have some bearing on the share of shadow economy. The share of corporate sector should have some bearing on determining the share of shadow economy. But none of these structural factors mattered in the econometric equation determining the size of the shadow economy in the Schneider paper.

It is little wonder that the results had some surprising features. The country that came out with having the lowest share of shadow economy in developing countries was China, lower than Singapore's! India seemed to have fairly moderate level of shadow economy, much smaller than Sri Lanka's.

The process as well as the product of the World Bank study raises some doubts about the scientific content of the study and it is difficult to regard the study as 'the most reliable' available as is often asserted by eminent economists.

The basic point is that 'black' economy cannot be captured by techniques dependent on 'white' figures. I have seen from my childhood how black money is generated in businesses and how they are kept out of official accounts submitted by these businesses. There is no fixed ratio between black income and income reported to tax authorities in any sector. Trying to estimate black money from white data is thus basically futile. What we need is to draw upon the knowledge of insiders of the pockets that generate black money: an investigative approach in the tradition of Sherlock Holmes rather than a so-called scientific approach in the tradition of Newton. Perhaps the authorities interested in estimating the size of black economy should try to get together some senior citizens (who are no longer in active business and can hopefully speak honestly), chartered accountants, real estate dealers, jewellery makers and traders, hawala experts, tax officials, lawyers and erstwhile judges to form a committee to review the problem of black money and come up with suggestions on the cure.

In the meantime, the only way to get in the open all the black money that has been generated, legally or illegally, is to force the holders of all types of money to exchange their holdings for new money and penalise those who cannot explain the source of their money. Wanchoo Committee set up in 1970 by the Ministry of Finance to deal with reform of direct taxes was wise enough to recommend in its interim report in 1970 that demonetisation was the way to bring out black money. However, it was India's misfortune that this recommendation was not acted upon for political reasons. In 1971, Prime Minister Indira Gandhi rejected Wanchoo Committee's recommendation on demonetisation for fear of adverse electoral consequences. Political leaders on the left from Ram Manohar Lohia to Jyoti Basu had been arguing for an action against black money. But even when the Congress leaned to the left, it was unable or unwilling to act.

White Paper on Black Money: A Non-event

Under pressure from the public to do something about corruption and black money, the UPA government initiated in 2011 three studies on black money under three economic research institutes and while waiting for these reports, it published a 'White Paper on Black Money' in 2012. It is strange that the reports have not been made public even after four years of their submission. The rumour mill has it that the findings of these reports were inconvenient to the then government.

The White Paper goes over the literature on estimates of black money in India. It begins with the obvious point that there is no agreed methodology on defining black economy or black money and of course no agreed numbers on the size of black money. It refers to a World Bank study which concluded that

> [T]he weighted average size of the shadow economy (as a percentage of 'official' GDP) of these 162 countries in 2007 was 31 per cent as compared to 34 per cent in 1999. For India, these figures were 20.7 per cent and 23.2 per cent respectively.

The clear implication was that the problem was less serious in India than in its comparators and it was becoming less serious over time!

With such a reassuring picture on black economy and black money, why bother to draw up an action plan to curb the menace? Just for bureaucratic purpose, the White Paper had to write about 'The Way Forward' for tackling the problem with a section that covers 19 pages. It left no stone unturned. It touched on the issues of rationalisation of tax rates, reducing transaction costs of compliance and administration and further economic liberalisation. It looked in turn at reforms in all the major vulnerable sectors of the economy: financial sector, real estate, bullion and jewellery sector, mining and allocation of property rights over natural resources, equity trading, misuse of corporate structure for generation of black money, non-profit organisations and the cooperative sector. It covered as many as 13 items for creating effective credible deterrence which included integration of databases leading to actionable intelligence by monitoring agencies, strategies to strengthen direct tax administration, strengthening of the prosecution mechanism, enhanced exchange of information, income tax overseas units, efforts to be undertaken at international forums, international taxation and transfer pricing, effective curbing of structuring through tax havens, strengthening of indirect tax administration and steps to curb generation of black money within India. It talked of strategies for curbing generation of black money through illegal or criminal activities and of strategies for repatriation of black money stashed abroad.

A critical review of the White Paper clearly shows its casual treatment of the subject. It made a mechanical review of the literature on black money without highlighting the trends it showed. And then it went on to produce a long laundry list of the measures to be taken without any strategic thrust or focus on time-bound actions. With such a long and unfocused list of proposed actions, in reality no strategic action could be taken, and none was, during the following two years of the regime.

New Environment for Tackling Black Money

Fortunately, with a clear majority in Lok Sabha given by the electorate to Bharatiya Janata Party (BJP) in 2014, the compulsions of coalition dharma were relaxed. And India was fortunate to have a leader like Modi, who with his business background understood the validity of Santhanam-cum-Wanchoo Committee and was prepared to act upon them despite electoral risks and announced his historic decision on demonetisation on 8 November 2016.

The 8th November announcement is referred to as demonetisation, though strictly speaking it was not so.

Demonetisation means that some currency unit loses its legal tender. Demonetisation of notes of ₹1,000, ₹5,000 and ₹10,000 was done in 1978 first by an ordinance and then by the High

Denomination Bank Notes (Demonetisation) Act, 1978. What was done on 8 November 2016 was not to declare ₹500 and ₹1,000 notes as losing legal tender status but to cease circulation with some exceptions. All these notes could be deposited in banks and other designated agencies and converted into new notes over time. Thus, it was a case of *note badli* (change of notes), not *note bandi* (end of notes), though the opposition parties and many in media continued to use the emotive word *notebandi*, evoking the memory of the draconian *nasbandi* (sterilisation) programme under Sanjay Gandhi in the 1970s.

This was not the first time such an action had been taken in India. First case of demonetisation in India was on 12 January 1946. Banknotes of ₹1,000 and ₹10,000 were withdrawn and new notes of ₹1,000, ₹5,000 and ₹10,000 were introduced in 1954. Out of a total issue of ₹143.97 crore of high-denomination notes, ₹134.9 crore were exchanged. Thus, only about ₹9.07 crore were demonetised.

In 1978, banknotes of ₹1,000, ₹5,000 and ₹10,000 were demonetised with a view to curb counterfeiting and black money. High denomination formed only about 0.6 per cent of the total currency in circulation. Out of ₹146 crore of high-denomination notes in circulation, ₹125 crore were surrendered to the Reserve Bank of India (RBI), which meant about 15 per cent of notes were evaporated. The 1978 exercise was on a small scale and it did not create any great waves. The then governor of RBI had reportedly expressed scepticism about the success of the project. He had pointed out that the people who had substantial amount of black money rarely kept it in cash and to the extent they held it in cash they could find agents to convert these black notes into white through a series of small transactions which could not be called into question. The measure did not root out black money. In fact, black money grew faster than ever in the period that followed.

Some Facts and Figures Relevant for Assessing Black Economy

India is an unusually cash-oriented economy. According to a study done by Institute for Business in the Global Context published in 2015, the value of currency in circulation as a percentage of GDP was 12.04 compared to 3.93 in Brazil, 5.32 in Mexico and 3.72 in South Africa.

As of end-March 2016, banknotes in circulation were worth about ₹16 lakh crore, about ₹6 lakh worth in ₹1,000 notes and about 8 lakh in ₹500 notes.

While the total number of banknotes in circulation rose by 40 per cent between 2011 and 2016, the increase in the number of notes of ₹500 denomination was 76 per cent and for ₹1,000 denomination was 109 per cent during this period. High-denomination notes are known to facilitate generation of black money and form a large part of unaccounted wealth as found by enforcement agencies from time to time.

India is largely a non-tax-compliant nation where direct tax collection does not seem to be correlated with the income and consumption patterns of Indians. Out of 4.2 crore people in the organised sector, only 1.74 crore (about 41 per cent) filed income tax return as per the 2015–16 figures. Out of 5.6 crore informal and individual enterprises, only 1.81 crore (about 32 per cent) filed tax return. Out of 13.94 lakh registered companies, only 5.97 lakh (about 43 per cent) filed tax return. Out of 3.7 crore individuals who filed tax return in 2015–16, only 24 lakh declared their income as above 10 lakhs, while number of individuals showing income above 50 lakh was only 1.72 lakh. Out of 76 lakh individuals who filed income tax return in 2015–16, 56 lakh were salaried individuals. In last five years, 1.25 crore cars have been sold, while over

2 crore people travelled abroad. Assuming that a family must have an income of at least 10 lakh to buy a car once in five years or take a trip abroad, we find that the consumption pattern suggests some 1 crore of families with income of at least ₹10 lakh as against the figure of 24 lakh who declared their income above ₹10 lakh. This suggests a concealment rate of more than 50 per cent.

Only about 5 per cent of people pay income tax; the tax collection by the Centre and state combined is around 16.6 per cent of GDP, well below the emerging markets average of 21 per cent and less than half of the average of Organisation for Economic Co-operation and Development (OECD) countries.

There is much debate on whether black money is a stock or a flow. Clearly, black money is a stock, while black income is a flow. Every year, black income is generated and that can easily be a double-digit percentage of the official income of the concerned enterprises. The stock of black money thus created then circulates for conversion into various other forms such as land, housing, jewellery and foreign exchange. The stock of black money changes hands and some of it is converted into white money but at any point of time, the stock of black money is quite substantial. Anybody familiar with the world of black money would have seen almirahs full of hard cash with active transactions. Black wealth thus accumulated over the years is of course several times the annual black income generated annually. It is reported by the Ministry of Finance that on average, the amount of *cash* seized during tax raids of more than 23,000 warrants was only about 5 per cent of total assets of black *wealth* which includes not only money but other assets such as jewellery. These income tax raids showing the proportion of black wealth held in black money in individual accounts do not show anything about the proportion of currency in the country held as black cash in the black economy. The learned commentators who argue that the reports of tax seizures show that the black cash is a small proportion of the total cash in the economy are mixing up things.

The Argumentative Indian Overreaches Himself

Chapter 3

Most conventional intellectuals in India predicted gloom and doom following demonetization. But India's capacity for jugaad proved them wrong. Nothing disastrous happened though there was mismanagement of the process, leading to widespread distress.

Demonetisation decision was undoubtedly the most momentous policy decision of the Modi government. At one stroke, it affected the lives of a billion people without warning. Naturally, it unleashed a flurry of heated debates unlike anything else in recent years. In media, in academia, in club houses, in dinner parties and in street corners, demonetisation became a topic of discussion. More than weather, demonetisation became a topic on which one could start a discussion with a complete stranger and expect an animated exchange. It was perfect grist to the minds of argumentative Indians.

A Despotic Act Leading to Loss of Trust in Money

Amartya Sen called demonetisation a 'despotic action that has struck at the root of economy based on trust'. 'It (demonetisation) undermines notes, it undermines bank accounts, it undermines the entire economy of trust. That is the sense in which it is despotic'.

Under normal circumstances, one will have to take the comments of an eminent person like Amartya Sen seriously. But his comments on demonetisation are mystifying. Such an important decision cannot be taken through Parliamentary debates or referendum. Secrecy is essential for its success. If anticipated, the holders of black money will design instruments of money laundering including leakages abroad and there might be a risk of serious decline in value of the currency and hyperinflation. As in 1978, when demonetisation was done, the current decision was an executive decision by a duly elected government. There had been consultations with key officials over many months and the decision was taken after due deliberations. It is interesting that none of the political leaders in the opposition highly critical of demonetisation have called it despotic or anti-democratic. There seems no basis for calling demonetisation decision despotic.

There was no breach of trust because the so-called demonetisation exercise does not deny the validity of the claim of the holder of currency. His/her claim is safe in the form of bank deposits, except to the extent that the holder has money whose source cannot be explained when required to do so. Restrictions of the pace of withdrawal are common in the use of automatic teller machines (ATMs) and for large withdrawals when necessary in public interest. Again there is no sign of public showing lack of trust in the Indian currency. Nor is there any sign of flight to foreign currency. In fact, rupee has been appreciating vis-à-vis US dollar.

Not Fully Legal

In legally alert India, there have been public interest litigations questioning the legality of demonetisation. There are at least five arguments on which the legality and constitutional validity of demonetisation have been challenged.

First and foremost, the very constitutionality of Section 26(2) of the Reserve Bank of India Act, 1934, under which the union government is given the power to declare that any note issued by RBI will no longer be legal tender is assailed on the grounds of 'excessive delegation'.

Second, it is argued that the precedent of 1978—The High Denomination Bank Notes (Demonetisation) Act, 1978 repealing the High Denomination Bank Notes (Demonetisation) Ordinance 1978—and Section 26A of the RBI Act clearly suggest that demonetisation of this scale with such a draconian effect can only be done by a statute of Parliament and that was not done in the present case.

Third, it is argued that the 8 November notification was a hasty decision, taken without appreciating all the issues, and was causing prejudice and inconvenience to the public at large.

The fourth contention is that the central board of RBI did not give a recommendation independently after detailed consideration of all the issues, although the same was elicited by the central government. The RBI Act, the petition says, uses the phrase 'recommendation' and not 'consultation', and therefore a recommendation from RBI cannot emanate from the central government itself.

Fifth, there is the issue of correlation between reasonableness of a legislation or an executive decision and its immediate effect, as held by the Supreme Court in a judgement rendered by the constitution bench in 1954 (*Saghir Ahmad v State of Uttar Pradesh*). Although the Supreme Court's judgement pointing to such correlation was rendered in the context of legislation, the petition argues that 'the test that applies to legislation would apply more vigorously to executive decisions within the precincts of a statute'.

During the arguments in the Supreme Court on 15 November, Attorney General Mukul Rohatgi distinguished demonetisation from the declaration that currency notes of a certain denomination cease to be a legal tender, saying while the former would require amending the RBI Act, the latter could be achieved through a gazette notification.

This is because demonetisation would make even the keeping of a currency note which is not legal tender an offence and, therefore, for depriving the freedom of citizens, recourse to law is a must.

Rohatgi told the court that demonetisation would take its legal form once the RBI Act is amended, in due course, after the last date for exchange of old notes is over, so as to make it an offence to keep the illegal tender.

The non-recourse to the amendment of the RBI Act was because of the need to ensure confidentiality until the decision was taken, consistent with its objects—fight corruption, black money and financing of terrorism through counterfeiting of currency notes—he explained.

The Supreme Court has considered the arguments presented above and refused to intervene beyond asking the government to do its best to address the hardships caused by the decision to particular sections. After the Supreme Court's decision, the legal case can be regarded as closed.

Damaging the Hard-earned Autonomy of RBI

A third line of criticism is that RBI, which issues the banknotes, was not given due voice in the decision and was rushed into action without adequate preparation. It appears that the RBI board was called to New Delhi one day before the announcement on 8 November to sign off on the decision taken by the government. There is no evidence of deliberations by the members of the

RBI board on the pros and cons of the decision and on ways and means of implementing the decision effectively. Three days before the announcement, banks were only told that they would be receiving new banknotes. At the Cabinet meeting before Modi's announcement, ministers were told to keep their mobile phones outside the room and reports suggest that they were not allowed to leave until the PM's decision had been broadcast.

The move was announced and administered overnight and that impacted the banking system's ability to ensure a smooth transition. Several ATMs across the nation continued to be useless by virtue of not having enough fresh notes, while the ones that were refilled were attacked by painfully long lines and eventually emptied at once.

The governor of RBI has stated in front of the Parliamentary Committee and elsewhere that deliberations on demonetisation between the government and RBI have been going on for quite some time. The statements of the governor do not clarify if there were open-minded discussions or more of instructions from the government. Nor is it clear if the involvement was only of the governor or of the board. The general impression is that the government leadership was highly distrustful of its colleagues and partners in the government and RBI in the name of secrecy and it failed to make adequate preparations for this momentous decision. It has been rightly pointed out that in connection with preparation of budget every year, scores of officials are involved without any problem on account of secrecy. A big decision like demonetisation should not have been restricted to a few selected officials.

Several commentators including some former governors of RBI have suggested that the autonomy of RBI was compromised in the decision on demonetisation. In our opinion, the issue of autonomy of RBI is blown out of proportion. Monetary policy is too serious a business to be left to unelected RBI officials.

The monetary policy has to be coordinated with other dimensions of macroeconomic management and the elected officials of GOI have to take responsibility for macroeconomic management which has big implications for the welfare of the people. Such a big decision as demonetisation which has had far-reaching implications could not possibly be left to decision-making or vetoing to the unelected officials of RBI. The emphasis on autonomy of central banks is a reflection of historical forces in the Anglo-American world and is not shared by high-performing economies of East Asia. Those in India who are obsessed with autonomy of RBI are suffering from colonial hangover and should learn from the demonetisation episode that such autonomy is not desirable in the Indian context. A monetary policy like defence policy has to be finally decided by elected officials with of course due inputs from the technical experts. (See Annex 2 for further elaboration of the argument.)

Some have argued that even though demonetisation was to be done, it could have been done through a gradual process. When the big changeover in currency system was introduced in European Union (EU) in 2002, there were three years of preparation in printing the new notes and making them available at exchange points and the conversion to new currency was done gradually. There are some experts such as Ken Rogoff, a Professor of Harvard University, who in his book *The Curse of Cash* has argued for withdrawal of high-value currency notes but over a seven-year period. In India, government gave only a 50-day window for deposits of demonetised notes. This was too short a window, particularly for people who may have been travelling abroad or residing abroad. A longer period would have caused less disruption and hardship. A gradualist approach that included the permanent withdrawal of large denomination notes would have served the cause better, even if it did not generate the same 'shock and awe' as the current policy did.

The government was guided by the desire to shorten the opportunity for money laundering by people holding unaccountable cash. Actually, however, it appears that 97 per cent of high-value demonetised currency has been returned. Thus, to the extent the purpose of short period for deposit was to prevent money laundering, it has not been achieved. This should have been anticipated and a longer period allowed to minimise disruptions.

Damaging Professional Reputation and Ability of RBI

RBI has a reputation for professionalism. But in this episode, it did not live up to its reputation. In 50 days since 9 November, there were 65 notifications from RBI about the procedures for taking deposits, giving out cash, etc. On several occasions, there were changes within the same day. This caused great confusion among the public and put the whole process in disrepute.

On 8 November, Prime Minister Narendra Modi announced that old notes worth ₹4,000 could be exchanged at banks and old notes would still be valid at fuel stations, airports and railway stations. One day later, the government ordered Metro stations, monuments under the Archaeological Survey of India, toll plazas and medicine shops to accept notes of the discontinued denominations. Another day later, the government allowed the payment of educational fees using old notes. Any charges, taxes or penalties due to the government or the municipal and local bodies and bills for utilities like electricity and water could also be paid in old notes.

On 15 November, the government ordered banks to start using indelible ink for marking customers to stop multiple currency exchanges in a day but the practice was discontinued the next day. On 17 November, further relaxations on withdrawals were allowed for farmers and for weddings.

The government also asked banks and post offices to report to the Income Tax Department all deposits above ₹2.50 lakh in savings accounts and above ₹12.50 lakh in current accounts, made during the 50-day window provided to tender the scrapped ₹500 and ₹1,000 notes.

On 19 December, the government announced that deposits of above ₹5,000 in banned banknotes will be allowed only once until 30 December. In separate notifications, the Ministry of Finance and RBI said that over ₹5,000 worth of scrapped notes could be deposited in bank accounts only once, after the depositor has been questioned in the presence of at least two bank executives on why he or she could not deposit the amount earlier. On 21 December, however, RBI withdrew the restriction announced in the previous notification.

Withdrawals from ATMs were difficult. A simple example, widely shared, was that the new notes were slightly smaller than the old notes, which meant that ATMs were not set up to handle them. There were mammoth queues at any ATM that actually had any cash to give out in the form of ₹100 notes. Such queues were mirrored at bank branches where people were trying to swap out their old notes or deposit them. It was the absence of preparation with replacement currency, well-stocked banks and functional ATMs that turned this into an unmitigated disaster, rather than the suddenness of the change. A forward effective date known only to the RBI governor and the government could in principle had been kept secret.

The demonetisation decision was rushed without adequate availability of notes of ₹500 and lower denominations so that even within the limits of cash withdrawal allowed, the public was often given notes of high denomination (₹2,000) which were not usable for normal transactions of most people, thus effectively rendering the ₹2000 notes as illiquid.

It could be argued that the Indian case of demonetisation had no precedence in history. It was not possible to learn from experience either in India or abroad. Thus, there was a need to play by the ear and to use a famous phrase from the Chinese experience, 'cross the river by feeling the stones'. It is also important to note that many holders of black money were finding innovative ways of laundering their money. The government and RBI had to be alert to what was going on and change rules as necessary to minimise the avenues for money laundering. The staff in RBI and banks were under tremendous pressure to deal with the mammoth tasks of handling deposits, operating ATMs and dispensing cash according to the rules. They did a creditable job, though there were exceptions to the rule. Some amount of mismanagement in issuing circulars about the rules was understandable. As Prime Minister Modi put it in his interview reported in *India Today*:

> Our *rananiti* is aptly summarized by the age-old saying of 'Tu daal-daal, main paat-paat'. We must stay two steps ahead of the enemy. I had explicitly recognized that this was a battle against strong forces. When you fight such a battle, you cannot stand still and allow your enemy to gain advantage. If the enemy runs, we will chase them. If they change their tactics, we will change ours. When the corrupt find new methods of cheating, we will identify new methods to clamp down on the same. Also our government is responsive to feedback and suggestion from the public and the media. When problems are identified, we respond promptly and take necessary steps. Far from indicating poor implementation, this speaks of

DEMONETISATION: A MEANS TO AN END?

our agility in responding quickly and keeping up with the evolving situation.

It is true that given the unprecedented nature of demonetisation in India, some surprises were inevitable and some changes in rules as the process unfolded were natural. However, the authorities should have expected money laundering efforts on a large scale and designed procedures on the basis of detailed consultations with the experts. It is because of the inadequate consultations that precautions were not taken. Announcements of changes within one day were excessive and indicated mismanagement on procedures. It was truly a picture of a 'flailing state' hitting this way or that to check money laundering, an effort in which they largely failed. This should have been handled better. Dr Manmohan Singh was exaggerating when he called it a 'monumental mismanagement', but mismanagement it was. RBI Governor Urjit Patel's assertion that 'the decision was not taken in haste but after detailed deliberations' only suggests how poor was the quality of these deliberations among babus with inadequate knowledge of the realities of India.

Damaging GDP Growth in the Near Term and Beyond

Assessing the impact of demonetisation on GDP would of course be quintessentially an economists' job. Writing in *The Indian Express* of 17 March 2017, Professor Kaushik Basu, a former chief economic adviser of GOI, said:

> Just as a mathematician's ideology—whether she is a socialist or a conservative—has no bearing on the fixed-point theorem she proves, whether an economist is a communist or a communalist should have no effect on his analysis of the effects of demonetization.

Can the costs and benefits of demonetisation really be estimated with mathematical accuracy? Let us see the economists in their usual diversity of opinion.

Professor Basu in his article in *New York Times* dated 27 November 2016 said:

> With so much money in circulation suddenly ceasing to be legal tender, India's economic growth is *bound to nose-dive*. Another risk is that the Indian rupee could depreciate as a result of people and investors moving to more robust currencies. (Italics added for emphasis)

Noted development economist Jean Drèze said, 'demonetization in a booming economy is like shooting at the tyres of a racing car'.

Paul Krugman, a Nobel laureate economist, said, 'India could face significant short-term economic costs from the ban on large-denomination currency notes, with no significant long-term benefits'.

Dr Manmohan Singh estimated that as much as 2 per cent of GDP might be lost due to demonetisation.

The Economic Survey 2016–17 estimated GDP loss of 0.25–0.5 per cent.

Jagdish Bhagwati on the other hand said, 'This is a courageous and substantive economic reform that, despite the significant transition costs, has the potential to generate large future benefits'.

When eminent economists come out with such widely different estimates with none of them specifying how they got their estimates, can we claim that we are dealing with a science? Perhaps economics at this stage is at best a pseudo-science and in the case of demonetisation exercise in India, estimates of most economists have shown their prejudices rather than any expertise. And while the economists were fighting with each other in their ivory towers, the Indian genius of 'jugaad' was working in full force and proving them all—critics as well as supporters—wrong.

Soon after 8 November, anecdotal stories of loss of income started pouring in from state after state and from sector after sector with particular stress in agriculture, in informal sector and on the poor and marginalised people. Farmers struggling with drought in Tamil Nadu were further whiplashed by demonetisation. Kerala dependent on cooperative banking system was badly hit because cooperative banks were not allowed to exchange old notes for new ones. Jaggery production, plantation workers and onion producers in Karnataka were in bad shape. In seafood-mad West Bengal, fishing industry was in a state of near collapse. Beedi workers in West Bengal and tea workers in North Bengal were badly hit. A potato grower in Uttar Pradesh saw his bumper crop turn into disaster as price slumped. Wholesale and retail markets in Rohtak, Haryana, wore a desolate look in early December. In wheat-growing states of northwest, farmers halfway through the sowing season ran out of cash to buy seeds. The sales of two-wheelers, passenger vehicle and commercial vehicles slumped. Further, it is said that there was revenue loss to the real estate industry to the level of around ₹22,600 crore and the notional loss on stamp duty for the state governments was ₹1,200 crore. The sales volume and launches of new projects fell by 23 per cent. The list of anecdotes goes on and on. But what can we say about the aggregate effects?

Former Prime Minister Dr Manmohan Singh, an eminent economist, can be expected to have high credibility in his analysis of economic effects of demonetisation. In his article in *The Hindu* on 9 December 2016, he begins by pointing out that the Indian economy is not in a good shape: trade numbers are at multi-year lows, industrial production is shrinking and job creation is anaemic. Then he puts forth the prospect of macroeconomic impact of demonetisation being 'hazardous'. The nation, 'in his humble opinion', should brace itself for a tough period over the coming months. In his speech in Rajya Sabha, Dr Singh became a bit more specific. He argued:

[T]he way the scheme has been implemented will hurt agricultural growth in our country, will hurt small industry, will hurt all those people who are in the informal sector of the economy. And my own feeling is that the national income, that is the GDP, can decline by about 2 per cent as a result of what has been done. This is an underestimate, not an overestimate.

He did not specify over what period he was expecting this 2 per cent decline and how his estimate was obtained. If he was talking of decline in GDP in 2016–17 of which seven months had already gone, this would involve a massive decline (of about 5%) from the 'counterfactual' for the remaining five months.

P. Chidambaram, former finance minister, argued that the economy would take at least 18 months to recover, though again without any hint of how the estimate was obtained.

Economists at Ambit Capital cut their 2017 GDP growth estimate almost in half, from 6.8 per cent to 3.5 per cent. They thought the effects would last into 2018 too. Others made estimates of GDP loss of around 1 per cent.

Many gave dark hints of an impending disaster. Jayati Ghosh, C.P. Chandrasekhar and Prabhat Patnaik referred to what happened in the case of a similar but more modest experiment in Soviet Union. On 22 January 1991, President Mikhail Gorbachev declared 50-rouble and 100-rouble notes invalid as of that midnight with conditions imposed on replacement of old notes with new ones. The demonetised notes constituted only 11 per cent of the value of currency in circulation as against 86 per cent in the case of India. Yet the move proved highly disruptive. Inflation accelerated as did unemployment. Economic activity declined sharply. Some republics even talked of moving out of rouble zone and some historians link this move to the eventual disintegration of the Soviet Union. One hopes that Ghosh and her colleagues were not expecting a replication of Soviet experience, following Modi's monetary experiment bolder than Gorbachev's.

Ajay Shah in his article in *The Business Standard* dated 21 November 2016 darkly hinted at what could happen when money supply is suddenly curtailed. He argued that depending on how you define money supply, on 8 November, India experienced a shock to money supply of 86 per cent to 53 per cent. He then went on to remind us that in the USA in the early 20th century, mistakes by the US Fed led to a decline in money supply of 30 per cent from 1929 to 1933 which he claims triggered off the Great Depression! He declared that the loss of output due to cash crunch now cannot be corrected by cash infusion later. 'Macroeconomies do not work like that'. Demonetisation might well 'convert a temporary shock into a deeper, a more long-term recession'. Not just a slowdown, but recession!

Mahesh Vyas of Centre for Monitoring Indian Economy noted on 21 November 2016:[1]

> A steady stream of news reports of empty mandis, low footfalls at malls and drop in business in restaurants, stressed factories, etc. paint a grim picture of the effects of a sudden withdrawal of liquidity from markets. Trade bodies have made their estimates of loss of business. We estimate the direct impact on business in terms of the drop in discretionary spending by households. This alone adds up to more than half a trillion rupees during the 50-day period till end of December. Enterprise stands to lose ₹615 billion.

---

[1] *Cost of Demonetisation Tracker* by CMIE. Available at http://www.cmie.com/kommon/bin/sr.php?kall=warticle&dt=2016-11-21%2015:12:31&msec=360 (accessed 22 May 2017).

Montek S. Ahluwalia in his article on 25 November 2016 in *The Mint* took an intermediate position. The negative impact on the various sectors of the economy was bound to produce lower growth. His best guess was that GDP growth was likely to slow down to around 6 per cent in 2016–17. More importantly, it would also remain subdued next year. Since the slowdown would be concentrated in sectors which are more employment-intensive, the impact on low-end employment would be greater than on overall GDP.

Keeping up the economists' tradition of 'on the other hand', Rajiv Kumar pointed out why the adverse effects might not be so serious. He noted that all medium, small and even micro production enterprises (production MSMEs as opposed to wholesale or retail traders) surely have some access to formal credit sources. Farmers, he argued, can sell their kharif harvest of sugarcane to mills with receivables being directly credited to their bank accounts as always. Any amount of paddy can be sold to the Fertiliser Corporation of India at the government-declared minimum support price (MSP). Agro-inputs are normally available at 30- to 60-day credit to virtually all farmers.

As is usual for economists, attempts were made to identify the different channels through which demonetisation might affect GDP: demand channel, supply channel and uncertainty channel. First, demand has been adversely affected through (a) liquidity crisis, (b) wealth effect of lost access to black money and reduced value of real estate which often acts as a major store for black money and (c) the general fear of taxman for those who were spending their illicit income on luxury goods and services. Second, supply-side effects operated through loss of liquidity because the employers did not have money to pay their employees and because the loss of one product in the supply chain affects other products in the value chain. Third, demonetisation has created uncertainty about government policy on taxation and inspection and about future demand and thus on investment programmes. In addition to loss of real income, there has been loss of money income of farmers and other producers who have failed to find buyers and had to dispose of their products at low (sometimes below cost) prices.

As the situation unfolded, the critics were found to be exaggerating the effects of demonetisation on growth.

Due to the famous capacity for 'jugaad', particularly in the informal sector, many creative methods were found to minimise the adverse effect of demonetisation. It is constantly mentioned that the demonetisation decision meant withdrawal of 86 per cent of currency from circulation. That is too simplistic. For many activities, old notes were usable for quite some time. New notes were also coming in, cancelling to some extent the effect of withdrawal of old notes. Anecdotal evidence suggests that demonetised notes continued to circulate as acceptable tender among trusted circles. Some workers could accept demonetised notes for salaries and convert them at banks and through bank accounts of their own or of their trusted relatives. There were many retailers who were prepared to accept demonetised notes while giving backdated receipts. There are also stories that with the help of corrupt bank officials, new notes were obtained for a fee by some big holders of old notes and their urgent needs continued to be met. In the rural areas, most consumption needs are met by small-denomination notes, and demonetisation of high-value notes was not of much concern. Clearly, demonetisation did not bite quite as expected nor did it hurt economy quite as apprehended by the critics. The situation was just too complex to allow simple relationships between cash and economic activity that economists usually deal with.

Some sectoral developments were revealing as to how the expectations of economists were proving wrong.

As noted in *The Economic Survey 2016–17*, early evidence shows that sowing for rabi crops has proceeded well and many farmers could obtain seeds, fertilisers, etc. on loans. Cash income from Mahatma Gandhi National Rural Employment Guarantee Act (MGNREGA) of the unemployed in rural areas supplemented by migrants returning from urban areas provided another source of cash for rural areas. Agriculture, forestry and fisheries which accounts for about 50 per cent of the GDP in the informal sector (which accounts for about 50 per cent of national GDP) is likely to do quite well in financial year 2017–18. Whatever the counter-factual that analysts may compute, the broad feature of relatively healthy growth in rural areas is an important feature, alleviating concerns about demonetisation. The fact that rural areas account for 70 per cent of the population and of the electorate becomes of overwhelming significance in perception about the adverse effects of demonetisation.

All the speculative activities about the adverse effects of demonetisation were put paid when Central Statistical Organisation (CSO) came out on 28 February 2016 with advanced estimates of GDP for 2016–17, including those for the third quarter of 2016–17(Q3). The numbers surprised everybody, the critics and perhaps even the supporters. Even the Prime Minister was expecting some short-term pain. But according to the CSO, gross value added at 2011–12 prices in Q3 registered a growth rate of 6.6, with the following sector breakdown: agriculture 6 per cent; mining and quarrying 7.5 per cent; manufacturing 8.3 per cent; electricity, gas, water supply and other utility services 6.8 per cent; construction 2.7 per cent; trade, hotels, transport, communication and services related to broadcasting 7.2 per cent; financial, real estate and professional services 3.1 per cent; and public administration, defence and other services 11.9 per cent. Private consumption at constant prices rose by 10.1 per cent, government final consumption expenditure at 20 per cent, gross fixed capital expenditure at 3.5 per cent and exports at

3.4 per cent. For the year as a whole, GDP was projected to grow at 7.1 per cent.

CSO numbers are probably underestimating the decline in GDP and may be revised. But by all indications, the loss of GDP was not in the category of what happened during economic or financial crises in India (as in 1991) or abroad (the Asian financial crisis of 1997–98 or the great financial crisis of 2008). Certainly, the dark hints about nosedive in the economy or replication of the US experience of the 1930s or USSR experience of 1991 by noted economists (as mentioned above) are completely out of line with the reality.

While most commentators have concentrated on short-run effects on GDP, in our opinion, the long-run effects may be a more serious issue. Radhika Pandey and Rajeswari Sengupta in Uma Kapila (2017) point out a number of factors that can lead to protracted economic slowdown. First, there is the general factor of uncertainty about availability of cash and fear of tax authorities about explanation of deposits made and of current luxury expenditures. Second is the risk of some MSMEs going bankrupt with loss of activity due to demonetisation and failing to revive even when the effects of demonetisation wear out. Non-performing loans which are already a serious problem can get worse. Private investment which is already anaemic can also get worse. Demonetisation will have negative wealth effects due to decline in prices of land and real estate and that can contribute to slowdown of growth.

There is no room for complacency about economic effects of demonetisation. The risk of long-term adverse effects on growth has to be seen in the context of already poor performance of important indicators such as industrial production, private investment, exports and credit. Unless the government comes forward with an expansionary monetary and fiscal policy, GDP growth rate in 2017–18 and beyond may well slip under

7 per cent and we may lose our treasured reputation as the fastest-growing major economy in the world. The hope of moving into 8–10 per cent growth rate may also remain unrealised for quite some time.

Hurting the Poor Through 'Organised Loot'

But if demonetisation did not hurt GDP badly, did it have serious adverse impact on the poor? It is argued that some of the demonetised cash was held by hundreds of millions of the poor (including women without the knowledge of their male partners) as savings and for meeting contingencies. With demonetisation, they had had little to fall back upon. If the women brought out their hidden stocks of money, they faced wrath of their family and might end up losing their savings. The poor, many of whom lack proof of identity, had been facing particular difficulty in exchanging their cash. Many poor who were daily workers had lost jobs and their meagre incomes. Many in the informal sector had similarly lost jobs and had to return to their villages. Refugees, most of them poor, lack bank accounts and identity cards and had been unable to convert cash. Socially ostracised communities who are again disproportionately cut off from the banking systems—such as transgender communities and sex workers—were other immediate victims.

The poor were adversely affected but the surprise was that in a country prone to upheavals of the masses at slightest pretext, there have hardly been any large-scale organised protests by the poor against demonetisation, despite strenuous efforts of some opposition parties. It is possible that the poor generally have small savings in low-denomination notes which were not affected. In many rural areas, transactions of the poor are also mostly in small denominations and have not been affected by demonetisation. Many lost jobs.

But many of them had been standing in queues for depositing or exchanging cash for the non-poor and earning a decent commission for the task. Many of them were returning to villages where they are getting paid under MGNREGA. Thus, the burden imposed on the poor does not seem to have been unacceptably high.

Former Prime Minister Dr Manmohan Singh has called demonetisation exercise an 'organized loot, legalized plunder of the common people'. These are strong words coming from a person known for his sobriety. However, he did not explain how it was a loot, by whom, from whom and for whom. The present Prime Minister has argued that if anything, it was an effort to correct the loot by black marketers from the common people and an effort by the State to return it to the common people. On this count, the former prime minister seems to be wrong.

Hurting the Informal Sector

The informal sector is estimated to produce about 50 per cent of GDP in India, 25 per cent points of which in agriculture and the rest in non-agricultural sector. Despite enormous growth of the economy over the last 70 years, the share of the informal sector seems to have remained high, despite its technological backwardness and low productivity. This is basically because it manages to remain competitive with formal modern sector by avoiding taxes and regulatory restrictions including labour laws. In this process, anonymity is prized and cash is the preferred mode of transaction and store of value. Demonetisation by snatching away its mode of operation has dealt a blow to the sector. Anecdotal stories suggest shutting down of operation of many informal sector units for nearly two months in November and December.

At the same time, one should not exaggerate the effect of demonetisation on the informal sector. First of all, many in the informal sector have access to formal banking. Second, the power of jugaad is fully on display in the informal sector in the wake of demonetisation. Many used creative devices such as payment of wages in old notes in advance, use of various IOUs for transactions among familiar channels and use of cheques for those with bank accounts. More spectacularly as discussed in the next chapter, many creative ways were found for laundering black money and with remonetisation, many are getting back to the old habits.

Hurting Informal Finance

Pranab Sen in his article in Ideas for India dated 14 November 2016 drew attention to the risk of the long-term damage that may be done to the informal financial sector, comprising not only of the much-reviled moneylender but also numerous other institutions such as Nidhis, Hundis and chit funds. This sector according to his estimates forms nearly 40 per cent formal bank lending and will have a very hard time in exchanging its stock of currency and may indeed suffer a permanent erosion in its lending capacity.

Dr Sen is probably underestimating the capacity of the informal financial sector to survive as also of the informal sector in general. As discussed above, the famous jugaad will prove its prowess. But in any case, the informal financial sector is a vestige of old times with low efficiency and it is about time we move to formalisation of the informal sector, both financial and non-financial. To the extent that demonetisation helps in this process, it is welcome.

Damage to the Banking Sector

In their article in Livemint (1 December 2016), Rajeswari Sengupta and Anjali Sharma point to several problems that the banking sector is facing in the wake of demonetisation: (a) banks are not in a position to significantly increase lending, (b) their net interest income (NII) may fall over the next few quarters, worsening their capital position, and (c) their non-performing assets (NPAs) situation may get worse, further adding to their capital woes.

First, in the wake of demonetisation, the banks have received enormous amount of deposits. However, in the current context, banks do not know how long these new deposits will stay on their books. So they can deploy these only in short-term assets. Second, the burgeoning NPAs of the banking system have significantly eroded their capital base and hence their ability to lend. In June, gross NPAs (GNPAs) of listed banks were ₹6.7 lakh crore or 9.1 per cent of their advances. The 27 public sector banks (PSBs) account for 80 per cent of these NPAs. In 15 of them, GNPAs as a percentage of advances are more than or close to the capital to risk-weighted assets ratio (CRAR). Except for the State Bank of India and a few other PSBs, the CRAR headroom required to make new loans does not exist.

Given both these factors, banks will face constraints in using the new deposits to make new loans. There is also a question of demand for new loans. Corporate credit demand has been slow. The currency ban has imposed a big negative shock on consumption demand, which in turn may lead to businesses cutting back on their working capital requirement, at least in the next few quarters. This in turn will affect the demand for working capital loans.

If banks cannot make loans on these deposits, then they can either park them with RBI as reserves or invest them in government securities (G-secs). Banks would not prefer to park these deposits as reserves with RBI beyond the cash reserve ratio (CRR) limit, because these reserves do not earn them any interest. They would prefer to invest the deposits in G-secs through the reverse repo window. G-secs being sovereign bonds do not pose any capital requirements on banks, give them returns and allow them to match their asset liability profile.

The availability of G-secs in the market is determined by the borrowing programme of the government and is not easy to expand without raising fiscal concerns. This limits the supply of G-secs, using which RBI can absorb the excess liquidity from the banks. There has been no announcement yet on the expansion of the supply of G-secs. This implies that with more incoming deposits, RBI will soon run out of G-secs that are needed to absorb the excess liquidity. This seems to be the case because RBI has now made it mandatory for banks to hold 100 per cent CRR on incremental deposits. This announcement prevents banks from investing the incremental deposits in G-secs.

This does not augur well for banks. Their ability to make loans from the new deposits and earn income is already limited, for reasons discussed earlier. With the 100 per cent incremental CRR requirement, the possibility of banks earning risk-free returns by investing the incremental deposits in G-secs is also removed now. Theoretically, one option with the banks is to lower the deposit rates. However, even after interest rates were deregulated, banks have not reduced deposit rates below the level of 4 per cent that prevailed in the regulated regime. Lowering deposit rates below 4 per cent may cause a public uproar and it is unlikely that banks will take this step. Given this, banks will have to service the cost of these fresh deposits without earning commensurate income on them. This will negatively have an impact on their profits, at least for the next two quarters, which in turn will cause further deterioration in their capital position.

While the economists have been expressing all these fears about the banking sector, the bankers themselves have taken the demonetisation in their strides. Led by the State Bank of India, interest rates have come down and customers are finding it easy to get loans for cars and houses. In a recent meeting, the leading banker Deepak Parekh said:

There is a deep conviction that India will emerge as a much stronger force after demonetization. The biggest advantage for home-buyers will be lower interest rates, transparency and no large cash payments and thus, we also hope that many developers now move towards affordable homes.

In our opinion, demonetisation exercise has had net positive effects on the banking sector. Moreover, somewhat inadvertently, it has shown the possibility of a new approach on dealing with NPAs in India. Reference is often made to Paul Getty's quip: 'If you owe the bank $100 that's your problem. If you owe the bank $100 million, that's the bank's problem'. Before demonetisation, the banking system in India was facing a serious challenge of borrowers with large NPAs, many of whom were wilful defaulters. Various reform measures tried over the last two years were not producing desired results. There are now proposals for creating a bad bank which will assume NPAs, giving the banks a cleaner slate. But such an action would have a serious moral hazard problem and will be politically unacceptable with the appearance of bailout to capitalists who are under a bad repute at present and are seen as wilful defaulters. The amounts of capital required for recapitalising the banks and setting up a bad bank are also beyond the resources available to the government.

India's experience with NPAs and demonetisation exercise has shown a different approach to the problem. Under Basle III rules, the banks would need massive infusion of capital. Fitch Ratings agency estimates that the banking sector will need (with or without a 'bad bank') around $9,000 crore in new capital by financial year 2018–19 to meet Basel III requirements and ongoing business needs. But the Basle rules are mainly an accounting issue. What matters is the risk of runs on the banks and their collapse due to failure to meet the demands of withdrawals. In India, with the government ownership of most banks, the risk of runs on them is minimal and that is what has been the saving grace. As noted by *The Economic Survey 2016–17*, despite high NPAs,

> In fact, there has not even been a hint of pressure on the banking system. There have been no bank runs, no stress in the interbank market, and no need for any liquidity support, at any point since the TBS (twin balance sheet) problem first emerged in 2010. And all for a very good reason: because the bulk of the problem has been concentrated in the PSBs, which not only hold their own capital but are ultimately backed by the government, whose resources are more than sufficient to deal with the NPA problem. As a result, creditors have retained complete confidence in the banking system.

Demonetisation exercise has shown that under special circumstances, the government can regulate withdrawal from the banks with full guarantee of the safety of deposits. As former Prime Minister Dr Singh has said, in demonetisation exercise, the government has done something that no other country has done: restrictions on withdrawal of bank deposits. This is true but in the Indian case, it is done with full guarantee of the ultimate safety of deposits. Thus, the PSBs can pursue their programme of recovering NPAs with whatever tough measures are necessary of wilful defaulters without fearing a run on their deposits and without being excessively worried about accounting requirements of capital framed in an alien environment (by some international 'babus' with no concern with local specificities). It is interesting that European and American banks which were supposed to be complying with Basle Criteria got into a banking crisis in 2008–09, while the Indian banks which are not always complying with Basle Criteria have come out unscathed so far. As Sri Pranab Mukherjee has mentioned, the secret of success here may lie in bank nationalisation decree of Indira Gandhi in 1969. 1,000–9,000 crore of dollars that the government is supposed to provide for recapitalisation of the banks is better used for public expenditures (of at least 2% of GDP) to stimulate the economy. With slowdown in inflationary pressures, and increased revenues of the government following demonetisation, the government can pursue a more expansionary monetary and fiscal policy which would improve profitability of banks and of companies laden with NPAs as happened in the period 2003–07 when with rapid growth, NPA problem, worse than today's, was brought under control.

What demonetisation exercise in India has shown is that under Indian conditions, the government can devise its own India-specific rules to ensure security of the banks and allow them to go after big borrowers. The PSBs may thus have capital requirements different from those of private sector banks.

The fears of economists about adverse effects on banks were exaggerated and there may in fact have been some unanticipated side benefits.

Lives Lost, Time Wasted in Queues

Dr Manmohan Singh in his emotional speech in Rajya Sabha recalled his experience of long lines for rationed food during war time and said he found it 'heartbreaking' to see and hear of millions of poor Indians standing in long lines to withdraw some money for basic sustenance. There were reports of about 65 people dying due to heart attack while standing in long queues. There were also millions of hours lost with people standing in lines instead to attending to their work. Mahesh Vyas of Centre for Monitoring Indian Economy estimated that the households that stood in queues to exchange their old currency notes with new ones bore losses of ₹15,000 crore for foregone wages during the 50-day period.

The long queues for getting new cash and even depositing old cash were unfortunate. This was an unnecessary cost that people suffered due to mismanagement of demonetisation. As noted above, the emphasis on secrecy and surprise was overdone and there is no excuse for not having adequate supply of new notes before the announcement and not recalibrating ATM machines in time. The intention was good but mistakes were made.

The surprising thing was how the public took it. In a country where public is susceptible to eruption on the rumours of say somebody storing beef or carrying cattle illegally across the state, it was remarkable to see people of all ages, men and women, together, standing patiently for hours and not erupt in anger when at the end of the wait, they were faced with ATMs running out of money. In the book by Prabhat Pankaj and Sheenu Jain, Rajeev Sijariya and Rajkumar Teotia reported the results of a survey conducted by the government on 22 November 2016. The survey results showed that

- 90 per cent of the public respondents believe that the government's moves to tackle black money are brilliant / nice.

- 92 per cent of public respondents think that the government's efforts against corruption are very good/good.

- 92 per cent of public respondents think that demonetisation will have an impact on curbing corruption, black money and terrorism.

The survey conducted by the government may have had its biases. But the absence of protest to the massive dislocation caused by demonetisation was remarkable and called for an explanation.

The most common phrase that has been used to explain this behaviour is schadenfreude (pleasure derived by someone from another person's misfortune). But that was not enough to explain what was going on. Few saw any misery of the other. In fact, most black money holders managed to launder their money and most in the public knew about that. Perhaps what was at play was the public's deep revulsion about corruption and the conviction that demonetisation was a necessary step in the direction of purification *yagna* (Vedic ritual of offering to fire) as the Prime Minister was putting it. It was not just suffering of another person but also the hope for corruption-*mukt* Bharat that moved the people. This experience has immense implication for the future politics. While capitalism is acceptable, crony capitalism is not. While the government does not have to be anti-rich, it better be anti-corrupt rich.

Cost of Printing and Distributing New Notes

Several estimates have been made of the cost that the government/RBI incurred in printing and distributing new notes. Particularly because the whole process was unduly hastened, costs were high. Mahesh Vyas of Centre for Monitoring Indian Economy estimated that the government and RBI will bear a cost of ₹16,800 crore because of printing of new currency and transportation of new currency to bank branches, ATMs and post offices. Jayati Ghosh, C.P. Chandrasekhar and Prabhat Patnaik estimated the cost a much higher figure of ₹42,000 crore, based on the fact that ₹500 and ₹2,000 notes cost about ₹4 and ₹6 each to print and deliver.

These costs were unavoidable if demonetisation was to be done and they are not high in the national context with GDP of about ₹1.3 lakh crore.

Tyranny of Tax Officials

The government is clearly surprised and angry to see how wide-spread money laundering has been and very little of demonetised currency has failed to return to the system. As mentioned by the Prime Minister, the rules of engagement in the implementation period were changed frequently to stay ahead of the devices adopted by money launderers (*Tu daal-daal, main paat-paat*). Unfortunately, the government seems to have failed in this contest. Almost all the demonetised currency seems to have been returned and to add insult to injury, some counterfeit currency has also slipped in. Now the government's boast is that all that black money is in the open and by suitable taxation and persecution, it will show the money launderers who has the last laugh. In this mood, the government may well unleash a grievous form of inspector raj. Already thousands of notices have gone out asking for explanations for cash deposits above a certain amount. This may cause much harassment to the public without necessarily satisfactory outcome for the government. With so many options available for money laundering, no black market expert worth his/her salt will take the risk of depositing in large amount where his/her source of money cannot be explained. Moreover, at the operational level, the money launderers will be familiar with the low-level contact officers who will be open to compromise. Now that remonetisation is making progress, money launderers will be able to withdraw cash and make deals with grass-roots revenue officers in old cash-based methods. Even in cases where persecution will be initiated, money launderers will be able to use the slow court system to delay and even deny justice. If the final count from RBI confirms the return of most of the high-value notes, the government would have lost the game. The Prime Minister's boast that the black marketers would be having sleepless nights has proven empty bravado. The black money holders can say to the government, *Tu daal-daal, main paat-paat*.

It could be argued that the government will be using digital system to minimise person-to-person contacts. Those who can explain the sources of their deposits will have nothing to fear. Those with unaccountable sources of deposits will face penalties and persecutions without face-to-face contacts who they can try to entice.

In the words of the Prime Minister:

> Demonetization will in fact nullify the discretion of the I-T officer and remove arbitrariness from the fight against corruption. Taking this further would be the simplification of tax procedures and minimising the officer–taxpayer interface. The revenue department is building a system where the entire process of assessment is done online without any need for the assessee to appear before the officer. We are also making increasing use of modern techniques and technologies such as big data analysis and data mining. Through this, the selection of cases for scrutiny will be based on objective evidence rather than the whims and fancies of officers. The aim is to ensure that the honest tax payer is not harassed or inconvenienced, while the dishonest tax evader is efficiently caught and punished. Beyond this, any erring officer or banker will be caught and punished. My government has zero tolerance for corruption.

In our opinion, the task of identifying the launderers is huge and the government should not underestimate its magnitude and complexity. Here again it should not rely just on traditional bureaucrats (babus) but seek involvement of ground-level experts such as chartered accountants and businessmen to devise an appropriate mechanism for catching and punishing money launderers. And it has to be a multi-pronged programme involving reforms of bureaucracy, judiciary and police. No quick results should be expected. On current indications, the risks of tyranny of tax officials and their possible corruption are real.

Shifting Goal Posts

The Prime Minister in his announcement on 8 November specified the following goals for demonetisation: checking of corruption and black money, eradication of counterfeit money and catching the black money under use by terrorists and other anti-social elements. However, as the implementation proceeded, the government found modest progress in catching holders of black money and found that the incidence of counterfeit money and money with the terrorists was not large enough to justify the draconian measure of demonetisation. The government then kept on shifting the goal posts. In the words of P. Chidambaram:

> The Prime Minister realised soon that he had been convinced or conned to buy a lemon. He had no choice but to change the narrative. He propounded the idea of a 'cashless economy'. In his speech on November 8, the Prime Minister did not once use the word 'cashless'. It was all about 'black money' (18 times) and fake currency (5 times). By November 27, the Prime Minister shifted gears and in two speeches that day he mentioned 'cashless' 24 times and 'black money' only 9 times!

In our opinion, the basic goal of checking corruption and cleaning up the system of payments while checking counterfeit currency and terrorist activities remained unchanged. The specifics of methods for checking corruption and introducing alternative systems were changed with the evolution of the process as it should be while learning by doing. The government was right in changing the emphasis of the exercise as it evolved. There is no good reason why the first thoughts must be the last thoughts in a complex exercise such as demonetisation. The promotion of digital payment system (DPS) can be rightly regarded as an elaboration of how demonetisation would incentivise movement to a system where payments would leave a trail and thus reduce the risk of generation of black money.

Loss of Privacy in DPS

Former Finance Minister P. Chidambaram in his article in *The Indian Express* dated 25 December 2016 expressed his indignation that DPS will compromise on privacy. In his words:

> There is also another important issue—privacy. Why should a young adult be forced to disclose that she bought lingerie or shoes or he bought liquor or tobacco? Why should a couple be forced to leave a trail of a private holiday? Why should an elderly person leave a record that he bought adult diapers or medicines for his ailments? Why should the government or its numerous agencies have access to our lives through access to Big Data? I think these questions need to be debated before the country is pushed into embracing the digital mode for all monetary transactions.

Whether we like it or not, the world is moving to a digital era. In most countries, both developed and emerging, DPS is becoming commonplace. India needs to leapfrog to that. The issue of privacy is overdone. Even when a purchase is made in a store and a receipt is issued, a record of purchase is available.

Security Risks in DPS

Jayati Ghosh, C.P. Chandrasekhar and Prabhat Patnaik, among others, have highlighted the risks of security in DPS and how India is particularly vulnerable to cyber security. They refer to several related concerns: cyber security and possibilities of fraud and identity theft; dangers of possible misuse of private data, including by private companies; and use of data by political groups in power to oppress those in opposition. They also refer to a study by two US universities which found India among the nations most vulnerable to cyberattacks. These concerns are valid. But the question is not *whether* but *how* on switch to DPS. There is no reason why India cannot provide cyber security as other advanced countries are doing. We return to this issue in Chapter 6.

Puzzle behind the Ganging Up of Economists

Economists are generally known for disagreements among themselves. If you get two economists, it is said, you will get three opinions. But on demonetisation of 2016, there was, with some modest exceptions, remarkable unanimity of negative views among economists. Why was it so?

One possible explanation is that the tools that conventional economists have did point to a risk of serious disruption. Economists took demonetisation as a monetary experiment which reduced the supply of money. The standard tool that the economists have for analysis of the effects of changes in money supply is quantity theory of money which posits a robust relationship between money supply and national income through velocity of money. Velocity of money has always been regarded as being unstable in the short run. Even for long run, its stability has been questionable and the quantity theory approach has largely fallen in disuse. However, in the absence of any other tool, many economists expected decline in income in line with decline in supply of money. Their task was complicated due to the fact that demonetisation was only about some high-value notes and with lots of exceptions. There was no way of estimating what the reduction in money supply (defined as including both cash and bank deposits) was due to demonetisation. There was also no solid way to estimating the impact of demonetisation on income. But it is hard to admit ignorance and most economists rushed to adverse judgement in keeping with the reputation of economics as a 'dismal science'.

The other dilemma faced by conventional economists was that most of the presumed adverse effects were happening in the informal sector and their knowledge of that sector was very limited because of lack of data on the sector. The natural temptation was to scale up on the anecdotal stories of distress in the immediate aftermath of demonetisation without giving full credit for the capacity of the sector for what is called jugaad.

The economists' anger was perhaps further aggravated by the visceral distrust of most of them of the Modi government and the government's decision on demonetisation without any consultation with them. But events only exposed their emptiness and lack of understanding of the world of black money and the informal sector. Going forward, if the economists are to play their role in the development of the country, they must come out of their ivory towers and do some hard work to understand the workings of the informal sector where more than 80 per cent of Indians work. In the meantime, our political leaders would do well to moderate their blind faith in conventional economists and turn to swadeshi analysts who are better acquainted with the realities of the country but who have been marginalised in policy discussions.

Shortfalls in Achieving the Main Objectives

Chapter 4

Demonetisation exercise failed to achieve the big objective
of seizing black money and utilising it for public welfare. But
there were some modest gains in other areas.

No Sleepless Nights for the Black Money Holders

Giving sleepless nights to the holders of black money was politically the most attractive feature of demonetisation exercise. In his 8 November announcement, the Prime Minister said, 'The ₹500 and ₹1,000 notes hoarded by anti-national and anti-social elements will become just worthless pieces of paper'. It is this prospect of the corrupt getting its due that contributed to the common man silently putting up with all the inconvenience of standing in queues to encash its own money and manage with inadequate cash.

During the early days following demonetisation announcement, there were indeed anecdotal stories of cash being burnt or thrown in the river for fear of being caught with unaccounted cash. But there have been no reports of black money hoarders committing suicide or dying of heart attacks or having sleepless nights due to the sudden shock of realising their cash had become worthless paper overnight.

In 1978, when notes of ₹1,000, ₹5,000 and ₹10,000 were demonetised, 15 per cent of currency issued failed to return to the system. On the basis of these episodes, it was reasonable to assume that a substantial sum of money will not be returned. The 1978 experience would suggest that ₹2 lakh crore would be extinguished in 2016 demonetisation. Reportedly, the government told the Supreme Court that it expects to unearth about ₹4–5 lakh crore of unaccounted cash. Estimates made by economists ranged from ₹5 lakh crore to ₹2.5 lakh crore. Most estimates gravitated towards ₹3 lakh crore initially.

As per the 30 December 2016 ordinance, the unreturned notes will no longer constitute legal tender and associated liability of RBI will expire. This will mean an increase in RBI's net worth and the associated windfall can be used by the public sector for development.

Unfortunately, the government overlooked some vital facts on the black money scene in India. There are plenty of mechanisms for laundering money for a commission of 10–30 per cent. If the money is deposited through Pradhan Mantri Garib Kalyan scheme, the depositor will lose 50 per cent of the deposits and will have to invest 25 per cent in no-interest deposit for five years, which meant a loss of about 60 per cent of the deposits. And if the holder destroyed the cash, he would lose 100 per cent of the cash. The alternative of money laundering at 10–30 per cent commission was financially better for black money holders. There may be of course the risk of persecution of those found guilty of unaccounted money. But in the slow Indian system of justice, the violators can on the basis of past experience expect to drag the case in courts and effectively prevent persecution. In cold calculation of black money holders, money laundering was the most attractive route.

It is reported that most of the demonetised currency has indeed come back to the system. In fact, there is speculation that with the bank staff under pressure and unable to do checking for counterfeit currency, even some counterfeit money has been deposited. Thus, the money deposited may even exceed the money in circulation with a net loss to the system to the extent of counterfeit money accepted as deposits. RBI has not been publishing the figures of currency returned on the plea that review is going on to avoid double-counting. In these days of information and communication technology (ICT), the review is taking too long. The speculation is that RBI may in fact be facing an embarrassing situation.

Thus, although one has to wait for the final accounts by RBI, anecdotal evidence and the logic of the situation do suggest that almost all the demonetised currency has been returned and some counterfeit currency too. All the efforts at secrecy and denying time to black money holders to do money laundering seem to have come to naught. There may have been a major failure of expectation in this area due to reasons which could have been anticipated.

Holders of black money found many creative ways of money laundering. Among these are the following ways:

1. **Temple donations:** Temples which are supposed to promote spirituality and noble thoughts have become, in many parts of India, places known for corruption of all types, extortions and unhygienic conditions. In this episode of demonetisation, they were in the forefront for money laundering. Money from the donation boxes of temples are tax exempt and no questions are asked on *hundi* cash from temples. Money launderers gave black money to temples who could deposit them in banks and later exchange it for new currency notes, kept a commission for this service and returned most of it to the owner. Temple donations surged since 8 November. Even famous temples such as Tirupati, Mumbai's Siddhivinayak

and Kerala's Sabarimala temple had seen suspiciously large surge in their donations and their deposits in the banks. Some lesser known temples were openly offering money laundering services at a commission, sometimes as high as 50 per cent.

2. **Back-dated fixed deposits (FDs) in cooperative banks and credit societies:** Owners of black money had been able to deposit their funds as FDs in the names of villagers with back dates. They received new currency notes in due course, after paying a cut to those in whose name they deposited the money.

3. **Using poor people for depositing black money:** Money launderers were finding people who deposited amounts up to ₹2.5 lakh, below which depositors were not questioned. These deposits were withdrawn later and returned to the original owners with a certain cut.

4. **Giving loans to poor people:** Money launderers were giving interest-free loans to poor people who could then deposit them in banks.

5. **Finding Jan Dhan account holders:** Jan Dhan accounts showed a surge in deposits during the 50-day window (over ₹42,000 crore) and a part of it is suspected to be black money being laundered.

6. **Approaching the banknote mafia:** Overnight, banknote mafias had emerged. These were people accepting old ₹500 and ₹1,000 notes and giving back anywhere from 50 per cent to 80 per cent of the value in ₹100 notes.

7. **Paying advance salaries:** Businesses having black money had reportedly used old notes to pay advance salaries within ₹2.5 lakh limit for making bank deposits.

8. **Booking and cancelling train tickets:** Since old notes were being accepted until 14 November to book train tickets, there was a surge in booking expensive train tickets that people intended to later cancel and get refunds in new notes, with a small cancellation fee.

9. **Using professional money-laundering firms:** Run by chartered accountants, there are money laundering companies, which specialise in converting black money into white while evading the taxman. They use the technique of showing cash in hand, even when that money has been used, for taking cash for laundering.

10. **Jewellery shops:** Many rushed to buy gold until the midnight of 8 November, often with back-dated transactions. Jewellers happily sold gold at a high premium. Hands-on primers were circulating on how jewellers can do money laundering.

> Take your black money to the jeweller. He will give you a cheque back for the same amount less 4 percent. He will give you a purchase bill to show that you have sold silver utensils to him. On the amount of the cheque when you file your return, you will have to pay no capital gains tax as silver utensils are personal effects, and capital gains do not arise on sale of personal effects. There you go, the money is white now.

11. **Using farmers:** Since agricultural income is not taxed, any farmer could help launder money, from old currency notes to new ones, for a cut.

12. **Using political parties:** Since political parties can collect donations of ₹20,000 or less without having to reveal who donated the money, let alone their income tax PAN number, they became easy vehicles for money laundering.

13. **Higher education institutions:** In the bout of privatisation, many institutions of higher education have sprung up whose sole motivation is to make money. Many have recently made backdated entries showing large amounts of fees received from students, even when the students were not aware of it. With fees now running into lakhs of rupees, this channel can do laundering for hundreds of crores of rupees.

14. **Petrol pumps, medical stores and liquefied petroleum gas (LPG) agencies:** These were allowed to accept old notes and any receipt by them in new notes could be used to launder old notes.

15. **Paying in advance of rents and for purchase of cars and other durables:** With back-dated receipts, huge payments could be made in the name of rents in advance and for purchase of expensive durable goods. The seller could deposit these amounts with a proof of source.

16. **Payment of taxes:** From local level to the central level, tax payers were paying off overdue taxes in the old notes.

The above does not mean that there was no loss to the black money holders. They lost some 10–30 per cent in the process of money laundering. They had also lost some 20–30 per cent of the value of their real estate which was a principal store of value of their black money. That was however a small proportion of the accumulated wealth of the black money holders, not cause of any sleepless nights. Moreover, with remonetisation, deposits are being withdrawn and there is a re-emergence of black economy and black money. With the shock on demonetisation behind them, black money creators can assume that there will not be a repeat demonetisation anytime soon. They are going back to their old ways without losing much sleep.

Revenue Gains to the Government

There are multiple channels through which demonetisation was expected to benefit budget revenues. First and most important was evaporation of black money which will reduce the liabilities of RBI who in turn can give enhance dividends to the central government. The experts have discussed various issues regarding legal and regulatory reform that may be required. But one way or the other, the public sector would gain from the currency trashed. Second, the government will examine the cases of suspicious deposits and where satisfactory explanation is not available, collect penal rates of taxation. Third, with the painful experience of demonetisation, black economy will shrink, more and more income will be shown in official accounts and will yield extra revenue to the government in perpetuity.

The first source was expected to be the most promising. Even if evaporation of black money is as much as it was in demonetisation of 1978 (15%), some ₹2 lakh crore will be extinguished. As noted above, the government's early estimates were much higher: ₹4–5 lakh crore. But the current indications are that almost all the currency will be returned and the gain for the government from this source will be negligible.

There have been many high-value deposits. Union Finance Minister Arun Jaitley in his budget speech mentioned that between 8 November and 30 December, about 1.09 crore bank accounts received cash deposits of between ₹2 lakh and ₹80 lakh. The government is trying hard to catch the money launderers and thousands of income tax notices have gone out. However, as discussed in the previous section, there are dozens of channels of money laundering that have become available and which are compliant with the present tax laws. Any black market dealer worth his/her salt will not make high deposits in suspicious forms when so many laundering facilities at 10–30 per cent commission are available. In any case, at operational level, tax operatives will be familiar with depositors, and even with information technology (IT) facilities, the local operatives will have important discretion in deciding the cases. With their own black money hordes diminished, the local tax operatives known for their unholy ways may be open even more than before for compromises. In any case, big depositors can take to resort courts to delay justice. It will be a long battle and the government should not expect much higher revenues than in pre-demonetisation era.

Nor should the government have high dreams of enhanced taxation in perpetuity due to switch to official accounts on the part of erstwhile black money makers. Unless the tax system is changed, the attractions and old habits of tax avoidance will remain strong. With remonetisation, cash is available easily, and anecdotal experience suggests that dealers in the informal sector are openly preferring cash deals. They can assume comfortably that with the big bang of demonetisation with all its loud noises done so recently, there is not going to be any fresh demonetisation anytime soon. The hopes of sustained increase in formalisation of the informal sector without further reforms may be premature. There have been some increases in tax collection recently. But these may be payment of advance taxes in old notes as part of money laundering exercises. There may be a slowdown in growth in taxes in store soon.

A whole slew of measures are necessary to change the way of life of black economy and the government should recognise the enormity of the problem and design measures for the cure. It should also recognise that in the contest of wits between 'babus' with Western academic training and real-life operators of black economy, the former have so far lost. In a strange reversal of the position, black money holders may be telling the government, *Tu daal-daal, main paat-paat*. For design of effective counter-measures against black money, the government will have to reduce its dependence on 'babus' and involve the real-life operators in a big way.

Gains to the Finance Sector

In an article dated 26 January 2017 entitled 'Post Demonetization: The Investors That are Bullish on India',[1] Karan Kashyap has elaborated how many investors feel that demonetisation will lead to improved transparency and better business. He gives several examples. SoftBank's founder Masayoshi Son, who two years ago pledged to invest $1,000 crore in the country, spread over a decade, has in the midst of demonetisation reiterated his intent to stick and even to further boost his investment. Accel VC fund, known for being an early backer of e-tailing giant Flipkart and software firm Freshdesk, has raised its investment programme in India-dedicated fund InnoVen Capital, which in 2016 disbursed '$6 crore' and is targeting transactions of up to $7.5–8.5 crore. Private equity group Warburg Pincus, which has been in India in 1997, has already deployed $3.80 crore in 51 companies and may invest $800 crore in India over the next 10 years; this amount is twice of what it had invested in past two decades. Investments are expected to pick up as opportunities open up, aided by financial inclusion, the digital economy and migration from the informal sector.

These are encouraging prospects but as Karan Kashyap also points out in the uncertain global atmosphere, the investors are in wait-and-watch mood and no big inflows can be assumed in the near term.

Real Estate

Real estate sector has been the greatest beneficiary or the worst victim (depending on the way we look at it) of surge in black

---

[1] http://www.forbes.com/sites/krnkashyap/2017/01/26/post-demonetization-the-investors-that-are-bullish-on-india/2/#7d2402a1539a (accessed on 1 May 2017).

money in India. Black money is hot money and the owner would often like to pass it on to others through purchases of other assets. One of the most popular of such assets which can absorb large amounts of black money has been the real estates. Prices of land and real estate have been surging with increases in black money. This has created many millionaires out of the simple middle-class folks who had acquired some land in the earlier period and has been a bonanza to builders—big, small or medium. However, for younger people trying to buy homes for their new families, this has been disastrous. In India, in recent years, the ratio of house price to income in most cities had become much higher than it is in most developed countries. Such high cost of real estate was also hurting the export competitiveness of industries. In one fell swoop, demonetisation has led to drying up of hot black money and prices of land and real estate have been coming down. Some 25 per cent correction may have taken place already and another 25 per cent decline may happen soon which will bring house price to income ratio in a manageable range. As reported by PTI on 14 January 2017, HDFC Chairman Deepak Parekh said that post demonetisation, the biggest advantage for homebuyers will be lower interest rates, transparency and no large cash payments.

This decline in prices in real estate sector will of course reduce the profits and wealth of builders. But the builders have fat accumulated from years of real estate boom. Their carrying capacity should not be in doubt. Negative wealth effects for households sitting on their high-value real estate would have negative effect on their consumption, much of which was probably conspicuous consumption, a cut in which is good for the society. The government can also push the programme of affordable housing, including housing for all, by 2022. Housing happens to be a sector with strong forward and backward linkages and 1 per cent of GDP invested in housing could easily create 2–3 per cent of additional GDP. This alone will be a great gift of demonetisation to the economy and the public which the electorate may not forget at the time of election.

Lower Inflation

In his 8 November announcement, the Prime Minister said, 'The misuse of cash has led to artificial increase in the cost of goods and services like houses, land, higher education, health care and so on'.

As noted previously, the benefits of lower prices in land and housing are already evident and there are many anecdotes of prices of many agricultural commodities coming down due to cash shortage. Data released by the Ministry of Statistics and Programme Implementation showed that during December, prices of vegetables contracted by 14.59 per cent as against a rise of 10.29 per cent in November. Prices remained subdued for pulses category as well, with inflation for pulses in negative territory at 1.57 per cent as against 0.23 per cent inflation in November. The overall retail inflation rate based on consumer price index (CPI) was recorded at 3.63 per cent in November 2016 and 5.61 per cent in December 2015.

However, these were temporary gains and there are some signs of accelerating inflation rate. The annual rate of inflation, based on monthly wholesale price index, stood at 6.55 per cent (provisional) for the month of February 2017 (over February 2016) as compared to 5.25 per cent (provisional) for the previous month and −0.85 per cent during the corresponding month of the previous year. CPI for February 2017 showed an annual growth rate of 3.65 per cent which was higher than in January 2017 (3.17%) though lower than in February 2016 (5.26%). Thus, except for housing, it is too early to say what benefits demonetisation may bring on inflation front.

Government Effort at Whitewash on GDP Loss

The Economic Survey 2016–17 claims that GDP losses due to demonetisation are likely to be small and temporary. To its credit, it tries to elaborate how it arrived at its estimates. But in the process, it shows how fragile and pseudo-scientific its estimates are.

The survey is aware of the limitations of its methodology. It says,

> A cautionary word is in order. India's demonetisation is unprecedented, representing a structural break from the past. This means that forecasting its impact is hazardous. The discussion that follows, especially the attempts at quantification, must consequently be seen as tentative and far from definitive... demonetization represents a large structural shock so that underlying behavioral parameters of the past will be imperfect indicators of future behavior and hence outcomes.

To assess the impact of demonetisation on GDP, the survey brings out of storage the old quantity theory of money which has been in disuse for ages and which it does not use when assessing the outlook for 2017–18. It declares grandly:

> The standard way to do this is by employing the standard 'quantity theory of money'.

Under this equation:

$MV = PY$, where

- M refers to the money supply
- V is velocity, the rate at which money turns over (the value of final sales [GDP] per rupee note)

- P, the price level
- Y, real GDP.

Of course when it comes assessing outlook for 2017–18, it forgets the 'standard way' and says sensibly, 'Turning to the outlook for 2017–18, we need to examine each of the components of aggregate demand: exports, consumption, private investment and government'.

But problems crop up with the use of the quantity theory of money. The usual estimate of M which included both cash and demand deposits cannot be used because in demonetisation exercise, the total is not affected. Only cash is to be used in the equation. But even that is difficult because demonetisation exercise takes out only some of the cash. So, the survey makes some assumptions without explaining the rationale thereof. To quote:

> To calculate the effective cash in circulation, we need further assumptions.
>
> - It was assumed that 75 percent of outstanding ₹500 and ₹1,000 rupee denominations continued to serve de facto as legal tender.
>
> - It was assumed that only 75 percent of the ₹2,000 notes were liquid in November, improving to 85 percent in December and 100 percent from January onwards, as new ₹500 notes came increasingly into circulation. Projecting beyond end-December is much more straightforward, since the old notes are no longer circulating. Instead, the critical variable is the pace at which new notes and their denominations can be supplied (remonetisation).

All these assumptions and inputs lead to estimates of effective currency in circulation between November 8, 2016 and the end of April, 2017.

With assumptions convenient for their thesis, the authors of the survey proclaim their result:

> The resulting figures for effective currency in circulation are markedly different from market perception based headline numbers. These headline numbers suggest that the currency decline after November 8, 2016 amounted to 62 percent by end-November, 2016 narrowing to 41 percent by end-December, 2016. Our comparable numbers are 25 percent and 35 percent, respectively.

These estimates in turn yield numbers for growth in two transactions demand-related monetary aggregates that can help estimate the impact on GDP growth—cash in circulation and money (cash plus demand deposits). It is assumed that the increase in demand deposits for each month is equivalent to old currency notes deposited with banks netted out for new cash replenishment and any loan repayments. Effective cash and money are estimated in year-on-year terms, as follows:

- *Second half of 2016–17 (average)*: −12.5 percent (cash) and +3.5 percent (cash plus demand deposits)
- *2016/17 (average)*: +1.2 percent and +9.1 percent.

With these assumptions, the survey comes out with a politically correct assessment that the effect of demonetisation is modest: 'between ¼ and ½ percentage points relative to the baseline of about 7 percent'. If Dr Manmohan Singh's team were doing the exercise, they could have easily made assumptions to lead to 2 per cent loss of GDP. But the survey has to go beyond the short-term effect. It jumps, without any attempt at justification to the conclusion: 'Over the medium run, the implementation of GST, follow-up to monetization and other structural reform measures should take the trend rate of growth of the economy to the 8–10 percent range that India needs'. It is not clear if that is based on quantity theory of money or some other theory.

Estimation of loss due to demonetisation requires estimation of GDP with demonetisation and the counterfactual of what it would have been without demonetisation. It is too early to estimate the former and inherently difficult to find the counter-factual which would have occurred in the absence of demoneti-sation. In fact, the search for precision in estimating loss of GDP due to demonetisation is largely misplaced. What the Minister of State for Finance, Arjun Ram Meghwal, said in a written reply to the Rajya Sabha on 21 March is more honest and scientific:[2]

> The economic growth of a country depends on a number of factors including structural, external, fiscal and mone-tary factors (which is partly reflected by demonetization). Therefore, it is not possible to pinpoint the impact of demonetisation on India's GDP.

Push for DPS

Promotion of DPS has become one of the major objectives of demonetisation exercise. By creating shortage of cash, it will force people to use cheques and various digital payment devices. The government, it was stated, wants each and every transaction in India to be online so it can be easily tracked and taxed. Data from the Ministry of Electronics and Information Technology show that the number of daily transactions through e-wallet services such as Oxigen, Paytm, FreeCharge and MobiKwik shot up from 17 lakh recorded on 8 November when demonetisation was announced to 63 lakh as of 7 December.

---

[2] http://www.dnaindia.com/money/report-not-possible-to-pinpoint-impact-of-note-ban-on-gdp-govt-2361972 (accessed 17 May 2017).

With approximately 261 per cent rate of growth, these mobile wallet companies have witnessed an explosion in expansion. Since the announcement, MobiKwik has added 50 lakh new users. To further attract a customer base, it has launched a marketing campaign called 'MobiKwik Hai Na' (You can rely on MobiKwik) with front-page newspaper ads in five cities, radio campaigns as well as a company 'anthem'. The company is set to spend '$2500 lakh' on marketing and branding by December this year. According to MobiKwik's co-founder and CEO Bipin Preet Singh, 'This is a once-in-a-lifetime opportunity for us to capture the market and we will not let it go'.

Other than digital wallets, Airtel Payments Bank has also witnessed over 10,000 customers opening savings accounts within the first two days of its operations in semi-urban and rural areas. This bank, a subsidiary of the country's leading mobile phone operator Bharti Airtel, facilitates cashless purchases of goods and services through mobile phones, giving an impetus to the digital payments ecosystem amidst the cash crunch. As an attractive proposition, it is foregoing processing charges, offering the highest annual interest rate of 7.25 per cent and insurance of $10 lakh per account.

In December 2016, the government also launched two lucky draws—Digi-Dhan Vyapar Yojana (for businessmen) and Lucky Grahak Yojana (for consumers)—to incentivise cashless transactions. Winners are selected on a daily and weekly basis under the Lucky Grahak Yojana and weekly basis under the Digi-Dhan Vyapar Yojana respectively, leading up to a mega draw of ₹1 crore on 14 April 2017.

These are indeed welcome developments. But it also reported that as cash crunch is easing, the growth in digital payments is also coming down. Demonetisation by itself was only a one-time shock. Long-term promotion of digital system will require further actions which we discuss in Chapter 6.

Formalisation of Informal Sector

The formalisation of the operations of the informal sector will have benefits in terms of their improved access to formal finance, modern technology and governmental assistance in training and subsidies. This transition from the informal to the formal sector has been the case in today's developed country as well as in East Asia. With Goods and Services Tax (GST) in the offing, MSMEs are in any case shifting to the formal economy to take advantage of tax credits. If demonetisation helps to expedite that normal process in India, it will be a good thing. In a recent column in *India Today*, Nandan Nilekani, the former boss of Infosys Ltd and probably more famously the man who gave us Aadhaar, said as much:[3]

> India's economy is largely informal. But once a taxi driver becomes part of Ola, then in fact he (or she) becomes part of the formal economy. He is able to use data, get a loan, buy a car and start paying taxes. So the formalisation of a few hundred millions of Indians will spur growth.

Many of the owners and operators in the informal sector have now achieved higher incomes and modern education and are willing to adopt formal procedures provided the costs are not too high. The challenge is now with the government to design instruments for incentivising switch to the formal sector and punishing continuance of old illegal practices. For making India a developed country within a generation as is the objective stated by Prime Minister Modi, such a switch is necessary and demonetisation may indeed expedite that process. If the informal sector becomes transparent, pays its tax dues, honours its regulations including environmental regulations and pays decent wages and

---

[3] http://indiatoday.intoday.in/story/tap-entrepreneurs-for-formalisation-of-economy-nilekani/1/682637.html (accessed 17 May 2017).

gives decent working conditions to labour, it will be a great gain. But it will not happen on its own merely due to demonetisation. A lot of follow-up actions are needed and we come to that issue in Chapter 6.

Reduction in Corruption

Reduction in corruption is the central objective of demonetisation exercise. Corruption has become a way of life in India and is rightly regarded as a cancer. However, as discussed in Chapter 1, it is like a blood cancer, not a localised cancer. It cannot be taken care of by surgical strike in one particular area. It will need concerted action in many areas over a period of time.

Demonetisation by itself cannot be given much credit for reducing corruption. In fact, if tax terrorism is unleashed to catch money launders, it may end up increasing not decreasing corruption. Money launders when caught would have bigger incentives than before to avoid penal action and the income tax officials having lost their past hordes of cash would have greater incentive to make up their losses.

Reduced Corruption in Politics

It is universally agreed that black money vitiates the political system in India. Black money without any accountability is given to the political parties and individual candidates who can then spend it without any accounting and without any regard for the limits on election expenses imposed by Election Commission. The contributors of black money to political system naturally expect a decent rate of return on their investments, all of course in forms hidden from the public and official eyes. The adverse effects of this process on the probity of the governance are easy to imagine.

Demonetisation is expected to reduce the incidence of black money in the system. Parties and individuals with hordes of black money (often in high-denomination notes) will have to deposit them in banks and will have to account for the sources of these incomes. Those unable to account for their black money may lose it. For the future also, political parties and candidates will be able to receive contributions only in white form. A new system of funding through bonds is being set up. Under this system, the individuals and companies can buy bonds from RBI in their names through white money but then contribute to political parties anonymously. Thus, the needs for using white money and for maintaining anonymity will both be met.

Unfortunately, demonetisation and the proposed bond system would have negligible effects on the incidence of black money in the political system. So far, as stocks of black money are concerned, any party can deposit it in banks, claiming that it was accumulation of permissible contributions below ₹20,000 over the past periods. There is no anecdotal evidence that any political party has failed to launder its wealth and thrown it away. For the future too, the proposed scheme is toothless. Any individual can buy the bonds from its recorded income while meeting its expenses in cash from income (as is done extensively by many companies specialising in money laundering). Businesses and corporations can easily find individuals doing this job for a commission. Thus, political funding remains an area for full play of black money with all its deleterious effects on the society.

Checking Counterfeit Money

National Investigation Agency and Indian Statistical Institute estimated that in 2016 ₹400 crore worth of counterfeit currency was circulating in India which makes it about 0.022 per cent of currency in circulation. Demonetisation is too big an instrument for tackling counterfeit money. Usually, phased introduction of new currency with improvement in security features is the way.

In the current case, there are no figures on what amount of counterfeit currency might have been trashed. In fact, anecdotes suggest that under intense pressure for accepting deposits and changing notes, the bank staff was not always able to check for counterfeiting and some counterfeit currency ended up as bank deposits. Only when we get data from RBI on the value of old notes returned and the value of counterfeit currency detected shall we know the reality.

Checking Terrorism

Demonetisation is supposed to hurt funds for terrorists. Terrorists would be of course hard pressed to get cash from the banking system. But with the money-laundering channels discussed earlier, it is difficult to be sure if the terrorists like Naxals who could get cash from the public would not find intermediaries for money laundering.

There are of course no data on the subject, and no conclusion on success or otherwise on this component of demonetisation exercise is possible as of now.

To sum up, our assessment presented in the preceding two chapters shows that it was not a disaster as apprehended by the critics. But it also had mixed success on the key objectives of the exercise. However, the way masses put up with the pain of demonetisation might suggest that there was something in the process that was deeply appealing to them. Could it be the disgust with corruption in the system and faith in Modi as willing and able to do something about it?

It is possible that the exercise had some unanticipated non-economic benefits. First, it confirmed the faith of the electorate in the good intentions of the political leadership and increased their willingness to strengthen the leadership's mandate. Second, it exposed the inadequacies of ivory tower academics and babus. Third, it created the necessary political atmosphere for the big push towards making India free from corruption. Obviously, much hard work lies ahead and it is to these issues we turn now.

Gains from Unexpected Directions

Chapter 5

The demonetisation exercise enhanced the faith of the electorate in the present leadership for tackling the problem of corruption. It exposed the emptiness of westernised elite in understanding the complex reality of India and reiterated the need of decolonisation of the minds of intellectuals and bureaucrats. It also created a crisis atmosphere where big bang reforms can be undertaken.

Stronger Political Mandate

The political motivation behind demonetisation has been a contentious issue. During the general election of 2014, BJP had argued that there was a huge amount of black money stashed abroad. If they were voted to power, they would bring that money to India and would be able to credit a substantial sum of money to the bank accounts of lower income groups. In this context, the opposition parties see strong political motivation behind demonetisation. First, the opposition parties have been arguing that BJP in power failed to deliver on the promise of depositing the recovered black money in the bank accounts of the poor and it needed a substitute and demonetisation was initiated to avoid electoral backlash against the failure on delivering on the promise of black money held abroad. The government was assuming that a substantial sum of money in high denominations was black and that will evaporate when these notes cease to be legal tender. This money will accrue to the government and it can allocate it to the accounts of the lower income groups and that will earn it votes, particularly in the upcoming elections of UP in 2017.

Second, it was argued by opponents that BJP derived substantial sums of money from the big business in ICT sector and with a determined move to digital payment, it will help its erstwhile donors and prepare the ground for future contributions.

Third, it was argued that BJP was under the impression that several of its competitors in the upcoming elections in 2017 and beyond had substantial sums of black money and those will be rendered useless after demonetisation, thus hurting their electoral prospects. BJP on the other hand having inside knowledge about upcoming demonetisation would launder its black money and thus escape loss of its financial strength.

Ghosh, Chandrasekhar and Patnaik in their book *Demonetisation Decoded: A Critique of India's Currency Experiment* carry the motivation issue to a new level. In their view, it was not just an effort of BJP to steal a march financially over the opposition parties in the forthcoming state assembly elections. It was not just a diversionary tactic of the party designed to draw attention of the electorate away from the BJP's election promises in 2014 about bringing back black money stashed abroad and crediting it to the accounts of the poor. It was not even political economy under neoliberalism to bring huge cash in the banking system which will hurt the petty production sector by starving them of funds and helping the corporate sector with loans to expand their operations. It was not a means to an end but, to a large extent, an end in itself. It was a measure of 'shock-and-awe' tactics where very negation of rationality was its rationale. It was to project a leader who was bold enough to inflict suffering on the people in the name of national welfare.

Actually, BJP in power has been trying to recover black money stashed abroad and the public understands that its electoral expectations of big gain to common man from retrieval of black money abroad could not be realised. There was no certainty of substantial sums of black money coming to the government for distribution to the common man. In fact, there was substantial risk that the process of demonetisation would cause short-term inconvenience and loss of income to the common man and they would turn against BJP in upcoming elections. In fact, it was highly likely that many small and medium enterprises who benefit from black money will be hurt severely and since many of them are supporters of BJP, the government was taking a risk of alienating their core constituency through demonetisation. The beneficiaries of DPS are not just the big corporate but many small and medium start-ups with no special links with BJP.

The programme of demonetisation was kept under severe secrecy and there is no evidence of BJP knowing of it in advance and laundering their black money. Most opposition parties could and did claim their cash acquired legally under current rules of political finance and could deposit them in the banks.

Thus, the programme of demonetisation was launched for long-term benefits to the country in terms of checking of corruption, spread of DPS, checking of terrorist activities and neutralising counterfeit currency in spite of the short-term electoral risks. In the words of the Prime Minister:

> For us in the BJP, the nation is above the party. We have always lived by the principle of keeping long-term national interest over short-term political benefit. There is nothing political in the demonetization decision. It was a tough decision taken to clean up our economy and our society. If I were guided by short-term electoral politics, I would never have done so.

Narrow electoral calculations by themselves would not have led to such a major policy decision. Rightly or wrongly, the motivation most probably was delivering of what the electorate wants in terms of long-term socio-economic benefits and the electoral rewards coming therefrom.

Like Indira Gandhi, Modi may be assuming the role of messiah for the poor, able and willing to trample on the interests of the rich and corrupt. To some extent, Modi's demonetisation decision is comparable to Indira Gandhi's bank nationalisation decision. A narrative could be that the salaried and working class people are honest tax payers, while the rich exploit the system and accumulate wealth. The demonetisation is to redress the balance. This narrative combined with the image and perhaps reality of Modi being Mr Clean is a powerful vote-catcher for 2019. Thus, motivation probably included calculus of political gains, but not in a narrow self-serving fashion.

In fact, it is the opponents of the move that have shown their narrow political motivation in dealing with demonetisation. Ever since Santhanam Committee raised the issue of demonetisation, left-wing political leaders from Ram Manohar Lohia to Jyoti Basu have supported it as an anti-rich measure. The strident opposition of the left (in addition to that of the centrists) can only be understood in terms of their assumption that this was their chance to discredit the Modi government by presenting it as an anti-poor measure. The exercise which was about change of notes (note badli) was presented as end of notes (note bandi) with a view to draw parallels with the emotive and disastrous programme of nasbandi (sterilisation) initiated by Sanjay Gandhi in the 1970s. In their over-enthusiasm, they presented arguments which were clear distortions of the reality, extreme and empty. The poor and the common men with their intuitive understanding of the situation have rejected the opposition arguments and shown support to the government. Thus, it seems that it was the opposition which was politically motivated in the shrill critique of demonetisation and that has come back as a boomerang to hurt them.

Demonetisation was neither an 'organised loot' of the poor nor an economic disaster. The public gave its verdict through how it took the long queues and discomforts of cash shortages and how it voted in local and state elections since demonetisation. There was overwhelming support for BJP in these elections. The public seems to have bought into the government narrative on corruption and measures to punish the crooked rich. It also realises the need for a long-term mandate for the government to cure this dreadful disease. In political terms, it has been a clear gain for the government and a clear loss to the opposition. We may be entering an era similar to the Congress regime under Nehru after Independence. From that point of view, the demonetisation exercise turned out to be a huge bonanza to the current government.

The Prime Minister is reputed to have many virtues that make him uniquely capable of handling the task of guiding India towards prosperity with honesty. The virtues that knowledgeable observers point out are as follows:

- First, he seems to have an ethical and spiritual centre of gravity inspired by the philosophy of Swami Vivekananda.

- Second, he is both willing and able to work tirelessly in his duty.

- Third, he comes from a humble background conversant with the realities of grass-roots India but is fully tech-savvy and a dedicated moderniser.

- Fourth, as he says, he has no family obligations to worry about: 'mere na koyi samane, na koyi pichhe'. This is a very important consideration because in the Indian context, nepotism or support for the family is regarded almost as a family duty. And that has weakened the hands of many prime ministers in the past.

- Fifth, he has political majority and is not susceptible to what a former prime minister called coalition dharma of being soft on coalition partners.

DEMONETISATION: A MEANS TO AN END?

- Sixth, he has unquestioned leadership within the party.

- Seventh, he has a steely character which combined with political power enables him to say, backed up by his record of 15 years, that he will be neither corrupt himself nor allow corruption (*Mai na khayoonga, na khane doonga.*)

If he is true to his reputation, he is *better than any other prime minister in India's history to tackle the problem of corruption.*

The demonetisation exercise seems to have enhanced the confidence of the electorate in the Prime Minister's capacity to make progress on checking corruption and they seem to be willing to give him a long-term mandate for that purpose. This has been a major achievement of the demonetisation exercise.

Liberation from Ivory Tower Intellectuals

The demonetisation exercise has also exposed the limitations of traditional economists, media and officials trained in Western mode. As discussed in Chapter 1, they do not seem to understand the revulsion of the common man against corruption. Typically, economists are trying to make their subject 'value-free' science. Any reference to morality is regarded as out of bound. But in real economic life of the masses, morality plays an important role. In fact, economic life is impossible without certain moral code of behaviour. Typical Westernised economists do not understand that and monetisation exercise has shown the need for liberation from them if we want to solve our corruption problem.

As discussed at some length in Chapter 2, typical economists do not understand the black money phenomenon. They can only work with white data and relationships observed in white economy. That is not helpful for understanding the black economy. We need help from others such as chartered accountants, lawyers, judges and police officers who deal with that world. Thus, the next time the government wants a study on black economy, it should not commission economic think tanks but form a research team of the people familiar with the subject of their study.

More generally, our economists still seem to be suffering from colonial hangover. On many policy issues such as monetary policy, fiscal policy and trade policy, they seem to be looking for approval from the West. They need to turn their gaze to the realities of India and also broaden their search for role models by looking east.

Our bureaucrats are also trained in Western tradition and their minds also need to be decolonised. The procedures for selection of bureaucrats as well as their training should include material relating to the Indian realities and the values that drive the people. Instead of being largely a closed shop, bureaucracy should be opened up to induction of people with domain knowledge of the issues under consideration.

The demonetisation exercise has exposed the emptiness of our traditional ivory-tower economists and bureaucrats. Prime Minister's quip that hard work is more important than Harvard is a powerful signal for search for intellectual swaraj for our economic management.

The demonetisation exercise has also shown that unless there is a change of mindset about corruption, it will be very difficult to eradicate it. So long as the black marketers feel no shame in doing illegal activities, they will find ways of doing so. For change of their mindset, a touch of spirituality is helpful and the Prime Minister can bring that spiritual touch to his battle against corruption through his personal example and sharing of his thoughts with the public. In the good old Indian tradition, he may assume the role of what Rajiv Kumar in his book *Modi and His Challenges* (2016) calls Rishi Raj (sage king).

Using Crisis for Accelerating Reforms

The demonetisation exercise has shaken up things and created a crisis atmosphere which in Indian conditions may be a big facilitator of reforms.

It is often stated that India needs a crisis to make big reforms. There may be more than a grain of truth in that. The argumentative Indian loves to engage in debates and can always point out the adverse side effects of whatever is proposed. Paralysis through analysis is the usual result. This has been the case with governance reforms for the last 70 years. Whether it is reform of bureaucracy or labour laws or police or judiciary or agricultural income tax, reforms proposed remain mostly on paper. It is amazing to see how perceptive were the analysis and recommendations of Santhanam Committee report of 1962 on checking corruption and how far-reaching were the recommendations of successive Administrative Reforms Commissions and how little action followed. It is also interesting to note how the case for ending 'licence–permit–quota raj' was made during the late 1970s and early 1980s but little progress took place with points/counter points going on until the economic crisis of 1991. It is worth recalling that even with the major financial crisis, many argumentative Indians were vigorously opposing reforms. Reforms could take place only because India had no choice, as the then Prime Minister Rao said, 'decision-making is easy when there is no choice'.

It is not possible for an observer to say whether demonetisation decision by the current leadership was meant to create a crisis, minor or major. But it has happened. There is no point in endless post-mortem of the event. We should focus on where do we go from here? The crisis to the extent it has happened should not be allowed to go to waste. Prompt actions should be taken on reforms on which there has been a broad agreement over the decades.

In this atmosphere, we can start organising our thoughts on how to move towards a corruption-*mukt* Bharat with the confidence that if our ideas are right, we have a leadership that will dare to implement them, however tough they may be. It is to these ideas that we turn in the next chapter.

A Seven-point Programme to Achieve a Corruption-*mukt* Bharat

Utilising the momentum created by demonetisation exercise, the Government should draw up a seven-year programme to make India largely free from corruption by 2025 when we will be celebrating diamond jubilee of our Republic.

Defining a Corruption-*mukt* Bharat

Demonetisation exercise has created a political atmosphere for a determined march on the road to a corruption-*mukt* Bharat. The word 'corruption-*mukt*' has to be defined in a realistic manner. We cannot expect to have zero corruption in the society. Some amount of corruption will always be there as Chanakya would remind us. But it can be moderate comparable to that in the high-performing economies and societies around the world. In this connection, it is usual to define our goal in the framework of some internationally defined index, for example, when we try to define ease of doing business with reference to our rank in the World Bank index of 'Ease of doing business'. We can, by analogy, try to define our goal with reference to our rank in an internationally used index on corruption such as the Corruption Perceptions Index of Transparency International. However, that will not be a useful approach for several reasons. First of all, in this approach, we cannot even monitor our own performance. We have to wait until the foreign agency comes out with an index which is usually with some time lag. Second and more importantly, these international indices are constructed from the global perspective, and the indicators they use may not be the most important ones in our context. For example, the corruption perceptions index of Transparency International is focused mainly on corruption in public services and is based on perceptions of business people and other observers. In our case, corruption in the private sector is as important as that in the public sector, and we need more objective indicators. Therefore, we should construct our own index with components that we find important. The third problem with these international indices is that they refer to rank or relative position. Our rank may improve because some country has become worse over time. But that is hardly a consolation for us when we are trying to have a clean society. We need some measure of absolute level of corruption in our country.

An approach we recommend is to select a country which can be regarded as mostly 'corruption-*mukt*' and aim at reaching the level of corruption in that country in a time-bound fashion. The indicators would be grounded in our own reality and may be both quantitative and qualitative.

We need to do some review to select a role model. Perhaps Singapore provides a good role model. Even though it is small, it has shown a tremendous improvement since the colonial era. It shares many legal and bureaucratic traditions with us and it is easy to monitor. We can take Singapore in 2015 as the target and set a date by which we aim to catch up with that level. As discussed earlier, corruption in India is like blood cancer requiring long-term treatment and not a localised cancer amenable to surgical treatment. It is going to be a long march for us to achieve a corruption-*mukt* Bharat. Perhaps a realistic target would be year 2025, which would mean 11 years from the beginning of the current regime in 2014. Hopefully, the electorate will grant our current leader the necessary time to cure the cancer of corruption as it did for Jawaharlal Nehru, our first prime minister, to stabilise the roots of democracy in India.

What would be the components of such a corruption-*mukt* Bharat, and what would be the necessary policy reforms? It would be a big task which can only be done in close consultation with the common man. That is clearly beyond our capacity. Nevertheless, we will like to suggest some components which may be considered. We note seven such components.

Big Push for ICT

Around the world, ICT is revolutionising the process of interaction between different segments of society, government, business and public, and holds great promise for reducing transaction costs and ensuring greater transparency and accountability. In India, ICT is beginning to contribute to improving interaction between businesses (B2B), between business and customers (B2C), between government and citizens (G2C), between government and business (G2B) and between government agencies (G2G). Through what is called e-governance, progress is being made for better service delivery, greater transparency and accountability, empowerment of people through information, improved governmental efficiency and better interface with business and industry.

However, despite India's reputation as an IT leader, India's position in the international e-government development index prepared by the UN is quite low. It was only 0.3829 in 2012 as against 0.9283 of the leader Republic of Korea and 0.5359 of China and 0.4949 of Indonesia. It was, however, higher than the rank of Pakistan (0.282), Nigeria (0.2676) and Bangladesh (0.2991), as presented in Table 6.1.

Why is this so? Perhaps because business world of ICT has found it more profitable to focus on external markets and the government

Table 6.1. Rank Country E-Government Development Index

Country	Rank
1. Republic of Korea	0.9283
2. The Netherlands	0.9125
3. The UK	0.8960
4. Denmark	0.8889
5. The USA	0.8687
6. France	0.8635
7. Sweden	0.8599
8. Norway	0.8593
9. Finland	0.8505
10. Singapore	0.8474
11. China	0.5359
12. India	0.3829
13. Indonesia	0.4949
14. Brazil	0.6167
15. Asia Regional Average	0.4992

Source: UN (2012).

has not given enough support to promote ICT in internal management. Now things are changing. The Prime Minister has given clear priority to ICT, and the external environment for ICT business is turning adverse. With the rise of Trump in the USA, Indian ICT leaders are concerned about their business prospects in the USA. As mentioned by a prominent business leader (Mukesh Ambani), this adverse external environment may in fact be a 'blessing in disguise' if it helps the Indian ICT leaders to turn their gaze to the domestic market which has immense possibilities in the future. In the current context, we need to focus on two areas of reform:

1. Digital payment system (DPS) for all by 2025.

2. Digital monitoring system (DMS) for all MSMEs by 2025.

DPS for All by 2025

According to the government data, the number of daily trans-actions through e-wallet services such as Oxigen, Paytm and MobiKwik shot up from 17 lakh recorded on 8 November, when demonetisation was announced, to 63 lakh on 7 December (a growth of 271%). In terms of value, the surge has been 267 per cent, from ₹52 crore daily to ₹191 crore in December.

Transactions through RuPay cards (e-commerce and point of sale) were up 316 per cent at 16 lakh daily (3.85 lakh on 8 November), while in terms of value the growth has been 503 per cent at ₹236 crore (₹39 crore).

Government think tank the National Institution for Transforming India said that the volume of digital transactions in India had risen by 300–50 per cent since 9 November. The use of RuPay card has increased—in the number of transactions and value—both electronically and at retail level by over 200 per cent and nearly 500 per cent, respectively.

Paytm, claiming 1,700 lakh users, had a 435 per cent and 250 per cent increase in overall transactions and transaction value, respectively.

The government-backed payment app BHIM facilitated electronic transfers between bank accounts. Users could enter their unique 12-digit Aadhaar ID number to make payments. The easy-to-use system works on an ordinary flip phone—no Internet-enabled smartphone required.

There are plans to mandate digital payments at gas stations, hospitals and universities, with cash transactions over INR 300,000 banned altogether. Indian Railways will no longer levy a service charge on tickets booked online, and the government is removing duties on point-of-sale devices and fingerprint readers.

In December 2016, the government also launched two lucky draws—Digi-Dhan Vyapar Yojana (for businessmen) and Lucky Grahak Yojana (for consumers)—to incentivise cashless transactions. Winners are selected on a daily and weekly basis under the Lucky Grahak Yojana and weekly basis under the Digi-Dhan Vyapar Yojana, leading up to a mega draw of ₹1 crore on 14 April 2017.

However, there has been a big reversal in DPS usage with increased availability of cash. The increase in transactions in value terms in January 2017 over December 2016 stood at only 6.8 per cent. In February, in volume terms, transactions through electronic payment modes fell 21.3 per cent from 87 crore in January 2017 to 68.4 crore. In value terms, the decline was 16.7 per cent from electronic transactions valued at ₹97,011 crore in January 2016 to ₹80,765 crore in February 2017. In fact, the value of digital transactions in February slipped below that in November when demonetisation was announced. Even as February had three transaction days less in comparison to January 2017, the pace of decline shows that consumers have begun to move back to their traditional payment method.

Clearly, more aggressive measures need to be adopted, perhaps following the lead of NITI Aayog in using a lottery system for incentivising use of DPSs.

Universal DPS does not mean cashless economy. It only creates an option for a cash-light economy. The issues of security, privacy, etc. need to be addressed but should not be an obstacle to progress.

DMS for All MSMEs by 2025

It is widely understood that India can reap its demographic dividend only if it can find productive employment/livelihood to the youth who are joining the labour force at the rate of at least 10 lakh a month. Most of them have some modern education and cannot be absorbed by agriculture or old-style informal sector. They want decent work. Some argue that such employment will come mostly from the manufacturing sector. Others argue that with the spread of robotic technology, manufacturing will not absorb much labour. Employment will come mostly from the service sector including construction. The industrial sectoral composition of new jobs thus may be a matter of debate. But it is beyond doubt that these jobs will come not in the large-scale corporate sector but in MSMEs. It is also clear that these MSMEs will be competitive both domestically and internationally only if they have modern equipment and modern finance. The new crop of youths are better educated than their parents were, and they too will settle for nothing less. Thus, modernisation of MSMEs has to be the key for the future. And that modernisation can take place only if the MSMEs come out of shadows and have transparent operations which can provide the basis for fund-raising and international competition. It is unfortunate that despite 70 years of economic progress, MSMEs remained largely in the 'informal' sector because of the temptations of black economy and black money. The demonetisation exercise has shaken up the system. Now a time-bound programme should be designed to bring transparency to operations of MSMEs with regard to employment, finance, inputs/outputs and environmental matters. Such transparency will be needed for their prosperity and also for operation of GST and other programmes of the government. That would also facilitate monitoring of the economy necessary for sound macroeconomic management.

By 2025, it should be possible to monitor all MSMEs digitally. Registration will be compulsory for all. They would have a system of self-certification regarding their compliance with regulatory measures on labour and other inputs, safety measures, environmental measures, etc. Random checks for a small percentage will be made. Those who are found to be compliant will be rewarded with prizes and those found non-compliant punished.

Tough Action on Benami Properties and Wilful Defaulters

The Benami Transactions (Prohibition) Act, 2016 provides for tough actions for benamidars (a benami property or transaction means that the person who is shown as owner is not the real owner). Among its provisions are the following:

- In the case of the offence of a benami transaction, the guilty person shall be punishable with rigorous imprisonment for a term of one–seven years and shall also be liable to a fine up to 25 per cent of the fair market value of the property.

- Every suit or proceeding of a benami transaction pending in any court (other than a High Court) or tribunal or before any forum on the date of the commencement of this Act shall stand transferred to the adjudicating authority or the appellate tribunal, as the case may be, having jurisdiction in the matter.

- If any person gives false information to any authority or furnishes any false document in any proceeding under this Act, he/she shall be punishable with imprisonment for a term of six months to five years and shall also be liable to a fine which may extend to 10 per cent of the fair market value of the property.

- The central government may also appoint a special public prosecutor.

- A public prosecutor under this Act shall be in practice as an advocate for not less than seven years, and the special public prosecutor shall be in practice as an advocate for not less than 10 years in any court.

- The central government, in consultation with the chief justice of the High Court, shall, for trial of an offence punishable under this Act, by notification, designate one or more courts of session as special court or special courts for such area or areas or for such case or class or group of cases.

- The special court shall not take cognizance of any offence punishable under this Act except upon a complaint in writing made by the authority, or any officer of the central government or state government authorised in writing by that government by a general or special order made in this behalf.

- Every trial shall be conducted as expeditiously as possible and every endeavour shall be made by the special court to conclude the trial within six months from the date of filing of the complaint.

- The central government shall establish an appellate tribunal to hear appeals against the orders of the adjudicating authority under this Act.

- The appellate tribunal shall consist of a chairperson and at least two other members, of which one shall be a judicial member and other shall be an administrative member.

- Any benami property shall be liable to be confiscated by the central government.

- A benamidar shall not re-transfer the benami property held by him/her to the beneficial owner or any other person acting on his/her behalf.

The Bill, thus, seeks to change the earlier penalty of one–three years to rigorous imprisonment of one year up to seven years, and a fine which may extend to 25 per cent of the fair market value of the benami property.

Apart from the effective implementation of the Benami Property Transactions Amendment Act of 2016, the government may put on the Internet the information on property transactions along with the names of owners and value of property as is done in the USA.

Similar tough actions are needed for wilful defaulters who are clearly doing 'organised loot'. The size of this loot is now in hundreds of thousands of crores. An Act similar to what has been done for benami property should be enacted to punish the wilful defaulters.

Moreover, a system of naming and shaming can be developed by putting on the Internet the names of defaulters along with their specific misdeeds on loans.

Ease of Tax Collection

Complicated and porous tax system has been the major factor behind generation of black money and its spread through the system. GST will revolutionise the indirect tax system with transparency in recording of inputs necessary for claiming tax benefits and matching of suppliers and buyers' books acting as cross-checks.

A similar revolution is needed in direct taxes. The starting point is the recognition that ease of administration is a major consideration in design of such tax system. And informal sector is powerful enough to devise ways of evading taxes unless the cost of paying taxes is close enough to the cost of keeping the tax inspectors at bay. In this connection, the complexity and corruptibility of income tax system as well as its high rate has been well-recognised and is a key factor behind vibrancy of black economy. There have been suggestions from some quarters such as ArthaKranti, an NGO based in Pune, to abolish income tax and introduce financial transaction tax (FTT) as substitute.

That may be an extreme step. A moderate step with the same theme could be to have a modest and flat income tax of say 10 per cent on all incomes with very few exemptions and a significant tax on stock market transactions and international financial transactions. There will be a relatively high exemption limit for income tax of households and enterprises and above that, income of all sorts (whether agricultural income, or income from gift, or inheritance, or short-term or long-term gain, or lottery) will be subject to a 10 per cent tax. Anecdotal conversations suggest that many enterprises in MSMEs will be willing to forsake black economy and have white income while paying such modest taxes. This by itself will be a major deterrent to future generation of black money.

The combination of modest income tax with few exemptions and well-spread FTT will generate increased revenue with lower administrative cost to meet the needs of the State to provide public goods (particularly social and physical infrastructure) to deliver rapid growth with social justice and environmental sustainability. These can also be supplemented by heavy 'sin' taxes, some of which like tobacco tax and alcohol tax may fall in the in the territory of states while, while others such as carbon tax may be responsibility of the central government.

A major reform of direct tax system to supplement GST will be necessary to reduce temptations for generation of future black money. As in the case of GST, a considerable period of debate and discussion (focused on consensus-building) will be needed. But an initiative should be taken soon so that the new tax system may become operational by 2020 with the first budget of the new government coming to power in 2019.

Big Push for Expansionary Monetary and Fiscal Policy

It has been argued that the economy was in a healthy state in 2016 and thus it was the right time for a major operation like demonetisation. It is true that our GDP figures were showing about 7 per cent annual growth which is the highest among major economies, all of which are going through a difficult phase now. However, many have raised questions about the accuracy of our national income estimates and it is difficult to find other indicators of good health in the economy. There has been a decline in inflation and in current account deficits, but those were mostly due to sharp decline in petroleum, oil and lubricants (POL) prices which are now going up. Other key indicators such as investment rate, export performance, job creation, index of industrial production (IIP), profitability in corporate sector, balance sheets of banks and corporations and credit creation rate, all show a difficult situation. Taking a tough action against defaulters, wilful or otherwise, is causing disruption. In addition, demonetisation whatever its long-run impact has been a short-term disrupter. With drying up of black money, real estate sector and luxury goods sector are suffering setbacks which could be longer term in nature. The informal sector has been squeezed due to liquidity crisis and if remonetisation proceeds slowly and the government wants to keep currency supply below demand, slow growth in the informal sector will continue. In this climate, private investment in both formal and informal sectors is likely to remain sluggish. The upheavals in the international economy along with huge excess capacity in many sectors in China do not bode well for exports. Altogether, there is a real risk of the Indian economy settling down to low (below 7%) growth with little job creation for quite some time.

In an article in *The Indian Express* dated 9 April 2017 entitled 'We Need to Get Our Priorities Right. We Need to Hear Less Talk and

See More Action on Investments, Credit and Jobs', former Finance Minister P. Chidambaram has put on the table some inconvenient facts or in his words 'the bitter truth'. During January 2015 and January 2017, gross bank credit to all industries increased by a meagre ₹7,413 crore or 0.29 per cent. This includes micro, small, medium and large industries. That is why manufacturing (in terms of capacity utilisation or adding new capacity) and job growth are in the doldrums. Also between January 2015 and January 2017, the IIP increased by a mere 1.1 per cent from 189.2 to 191.3. In 2015–16, growth in gross fixed capital formation (GFCF) was 6.11 per cent. In 2016–17, the growth rate of GFCF declined sharply to 0.57 per cent. During the first two quarters of 2016–17, employment generation was dismal; only about 109,000 jobs were added when new entrants to labour force are nearly 10 lakh every month.

Mr Chidambaram of course represents a view from across the aisle. But there is some truth in what he is saying and unless something is done to change the situation, there may be some surprise in store for the government in 2019. The electorate may change its mind suddenly and if there is a change of government leadership, all the ideas about building on demonetisation and moving towards a corruption-*mukt* Bharat will be put to naught.

In this situation, every effort needs to be made to revive growth momentum of the economy and in near term, the most potent instruments are expansionary monetary and fiscal policies. In this respect, we believe that our policy-makers are slaves of some defunct doctrines from which liberation is needed.

For the last few years, the monetary policy in India has been guided by the doctrine that controlling inflation is the chief (even sole) objective of monetary policy and the view that the central bank can control inflation by raising interest rate. It is also believed that by announcing moderate inflation targets, the central bank can influence inflationary expectations and inflation. There has been no effort to demonstrate that these assumptions are valid for

Indian conditions. In fact, RBI's own data show that inflationary expectations do not seem to respond to its inflation targeting. Inflation in India has been to a large extent cost-push type and not sensitive to RBI interest rate policy. In fact, all these years, according to RBI data, the Indian industries have been suffering from huge and increasing excess capacity, which is hardly an indicator of general excess demand in the economy. All that the high interest rate policy has succeeded in doing is the slowdown of private investment rates, leading to slowdown of growth, reduced profitability and increased stressed loans in the system. By increasing the interest burden on the governments, it has also succeeded in reducing public investment programmes. Following this mindset, the RBI is now talking of moving from an 'accommodative' to 'neutral' mode, when it may even raise interest rates further in the future. This is a bad news for the future of the economy. There are influential and wise voices in the government calling for large (even several hundred basis points) cuts in the interest rates. But the RBI is a prisoner of its outdated and unproven doctrines and under the false theme of independence, the central bank is not responsive to the government's concerns. Unless the top leadership gets involved, this debacle is likely to continue with bad consequences for the economy.

Another defunct doctrine which enslaves the government is the doctrine enshrined in the Fiscal Responsibility and Budget Management (FRBM) Act. Following the doctrine current in European Community in the early 2000s, it puts a rigid numerical target on fiscal deficit, irrespective of what is happening to the rest of the economy and how the deficits are being financed. One important indicator of copying mentality of the proponents of FRBM is the Act itself. Vainly does one search for the rationale for the Act. The Act has some vague statements about importance of intergenerational equity, while in fact such deficits may be largely intragenerational transfers. It shows no evidence of the harmful effects of fiscal deficits in terms of contributing to accelerate inflation or adverse effect on private investment. In recent discussions, fiscal targets have become sacrosanct largely by referring to what relaxation in fiscal performance would do to India's credit ratings and financial flows from abroad. This continues despite mounting evidence of the weaknesses and prejudices of rating agencies and of doubtful contribution of foreign institutional investors (FII) flows for India's development. Perhaps a time has come when an independent minded and down-to-earth prime minister takes the issue head-on and makes bold decision on the merit of the policy.

To avert the prospect of our GDP growth going down below 7 per cent, an expansionary monetary and fiscal policy will be essential. On current policy, investment rate as percentage of GDP is likely to go down further in financial year 2017–18. Growth rates in consumption and exports are likely to remain muted, while that in imports may go up due to increase in prices of oil. The other markers such as job creation, credit growth, corporate profits, stressed bank balance sheets and under-fulfilment of the promises in social and physical infrastructure may assume dangerous proportions. Thus, in 2019, when the government goes to the public for vote, the opposition may well persuade the public to ask: are we better off than five years ago? If the answer is negative, public mood can change quite swiftly as the experience of Delhi election in 2015 showed. If there is indeed a discontinuity, all the structural reforms put in process with such hard work by the current government will be threatened, with grave consequences for the country. Thus, a switch to lower interest rates and fiscal expansion (perhaps to the tune of 2–3% of GDP) are must for the welfare of the country. Demonetisation has made that all the more urgent economically and perhaps all the more feasible politically.

The areas of possible expansion are many. Rural development and poverty reduction are obvious areas which are politically attractive and can absorb a large amount of resources. Acting upon the

DEMONETISATION: A MEANS TO AN END?

promise of housing for all by 2022 combined with digital system for all by 2025 could absorb 1–2 per cent of GDP with extensive backward and forward simulative effects. Social and physical infrastructure development has been starved of funds and can become sweet spots combining economic, social and political advantages. The specifics could be designed easily once the liberation from defunct doctrine is obtained. And there is no time to lose. If the switch does not take place by budget next year, it will be too late for 2019 and all the pain of demonetisation would have been for nothing.

Placing aside the misguided doctrine of the autonomy of the RBI, the government should decide at the Cabinet level (based on recommendations of monetary committee as well as fiscal council and NITI Aayog) what combination of monetary policy, fiscal policy and supply side policy is needed to achieve the macroeconomic objectives of growth with stability.

Reforms in Governance

The subject of reform of the government services has been a moot issue for years but with very little progress. The Tenth Report of Second Administrative Reforms Commission of GOI *Refurbishing of Personnel Administration* provides a majestic review of the history of administrative system in India and comes out with a comprehensive list of reforms needed. The current government can do no better than draw upon this important document.

The Tenth Report points out that the Indian Civil Services (ICS) on which our present system of administration is based was the instrument of the imperial power, and the leaders of the Indian National Congress had made it clear during their struggle for Independence that they wanted to abolish the ICS and all it stood for. Jawaharlal Nehru was 'quite sure' in 1934 that 'no new order can be built in India so long as the spirit of ICS pervades our administration and our public services', it being therefore 'essential that the ICS and similar services must disappear completely'. Yet in the years afterward, the ICS tradition not only survived but also prospered.

It is ironical that there has been no sincere attempt to restructure the civil services, although more than 600 committees and commissions have looked into different aspects of public administration in the country. Rather, the Indian reform effort has been unfailingly conservative, with limited impact.

The commission has advocated a total change, a radical transformation. It has proposed a wide-ranging agenda of reforms, which includes reforms relating to recruitment, training, tenure, domain competency, creation of a leadership cadre incorporating some elements of a position-based senior executive service, performance management, exit mechanisms, creation of executive agencies, accountability for results, a code of ethics and enactment of a civil service legislation. The key principles underlying the commission's approach to reform are as follows:

- setting right the asymmetry of power;
- insulating civil servants from undue political interference;
- professionalisation with stability of tenure and competition;
- citizen-centric administration;
- accountability;
- outcome orientation and
- promoting public service values and ethics.

The key recommendations of the commission are as follows:

1. For being eligible to appear in civil services examination, candidates must have training in core subjects such as the Constitution of India, Indian legal system, administrative

law, Indian economy, Indian polity, Indian history and culture apart from optional subjects.

2. Every government servant should undergo a mandatory training at the induction stage and also periodically during his/her career. Successful completion of these trainings should be a minimum necessary condition for confirmation in service and subsequent promotions.

3. Domains should be assigned by the Central Civil Services Authority (the commission has recommended the constitution of this authority) to all officers of the All India Services and the Central Civil Services on completion of 13 years of service. The Central Civil Services Authority should invite applications from all officers who have completed the minimum qualifying years of service for assignment of domains. A consultative process should be put in place where the officers should be interviewed and their claims to specific domains evaluated.

4. There is need to introduce competition for senior positions in government by opening these positions in government (including attached and subordinate offices) to all services. Also, applications to fill up high-level posts would be invited from interested and eligible persons from the open market and also from serving eligible officers.

5. The existing performance appraisal system should be strengthened on the following lines: (a) making appraisal more consultative and transparent; (b) performance appraisal formats to be made job specific; (c) performance appraisal should be year round and (d) guidelines need to be formulated for assigning numerical rating.

6. For motivating civil servants, there is a need to recognise the outstanding work of serving civil servants, including through national awards. Awards for recognising good

performance should also be instituted at the state and district levels. It must be ensured that selection for such awards is made through a prompt, objective and transparent mechanism because the value of such awards should not get compromised by either subjectivity or lack of transparency.

7. Accountability: A system of two intensive reviews—one on completion of 14 years of service and the other on completion of 20 years of service—should be established for all government servants. The first review at 14 years would primarily serve the purpose of intimating to the public servant about his/her strengths and shortcomings for his/her future advancement. The second review at 20 years would mainly serve to assess the fitness of the officer for his/her further continuation in government service. The services of public servants, who are found to be unfit after the second review at 20 years, should be discontinued.

8. Disciplinary proceedings: The minimum statutory disciplinary and dismissal procedures required to satisfy the criteria of natural justice should be spelt out.

9. There is a need to safeguard the political neutrality and impartiality of the civil services. The onus for this lies equally on the political executive and the civil services. This aspect should be included in the Code of Ethics for Ministers as well as the Code of Conduct for Public Servants.

For reform of the civil services, a review and possible repeal of the Article 311 of the Constitution of India is essential. Article 311 of the Constitution provides strong protection to civil servants against dismissal. The procedure laid down in Article 311 was intended to provide guarantee against arbitrary and vindictive action. In practice, it has shielded the guilty against punishment for abuse of public office for private gain. Such a provision is not available in any of the democratic countries including the UK. This has led to erosion of accountability and created roadblocks in reducing corruption. There is now a need for a comprehensive examination of the entire corpus of administrative jurisprudence to rationalise and simplify the procedures for ensuring accountability in public service.

The list of reforms proposed by the commission is impressive and should go a long way to improve quality of bureaucracy, if effectively implemented. Beyond the reforms of civil service rules, there is the issue of attitudinal change. In a democratic society, people are the rulers not the bureaucrats. But in India, colonial hangover is still persisting and is bolstered by the training on senior civil servants on induction and their early postings as virtual rulers at district level. As a result, the senior bureaucrats and even lower level bureaucrats look upon themselves more as rulers than as servants of the people. This was confirmed by no less a person than Justice Y.K. Sabharwal, Chief Justice of India, in his valedictory address (2 September 2006) at National Colloquium on 'Ethics in Governance—Moving from Rhetoric to Results' organised by the Administrative Reforms Commission and National Judicial Academy. To quote: 'The holders of public offices still treat the authority in their hands as one bestowing, upon them, the status of a ruler rather than one in public service'. This must change. The Prime Minister with his constant reference to being the first servant of the people has set the tone.

Reform of Political Finance

Demonetisation episode has drawn sharp attention to the fact that it is political leaders and their electoral machines that are the biggest beneficiaries of black money. They incur heavy expenses during elections and most of these are financed by anonymous contributors who in turn use anonymous money (black money) for that purpose. More than almost any other group, political machine runs largely on black money. Can the political machine really bite the hand that feeds them? Are political leaders really serious about eliminating black money?

Clearly in India, the political leaders have not been serious about controlling black money so far. There have been many committees reviewing the subject and calling for state funding of elections. But they have generally ended up denying such possibility on the argument that the economic conditions of the country do not allow such funding, without giving any idea of what the funds required are and how they compare with subsidies and tax benefits given to the favourites of political leaders. As we note later, the costs of elections and political parties in India fall well short of 1 per cent of GDP while amounts several times of this are spent on subsidies and tax exemptions. The real problem is vested interests and capacity of political leaders to check corruption on which they may depend.

But things are different today.

In his recent interview, the Prime Minister said:

> It is imperative that we figure out decisive ways of rooting out black money from politics. I have been regularly appealing for the same. I had asserted before the last Parliament session itself that the need of the hour is to comprehensively take a relook at and reform political funding. I have also repeatedly expressed concern about how our current system of multiple elections not only raises political expenditure, thereby hurting the economy, but also results in the nation perpetually remaining in election mode, stalling governance. We must think innovatively to break out of this continuous cycle of elections.

So when he puts demonetisation as a last but one step in the *yagna* of purification and reform of political finance, it is worthwhile trying to assist him by pointing out the success stories in this area and the possible line of action in India.

In this connection, the first thing to do is to point out that the USA, the richest democracy, which we often ape, is no role model for political finance. In fact, campaign finance process is thoroughly vitiated in the USA, and there are constant calls for reform in this area. High expenses of campaigns are effectively ruling out all but the wealthy for electoral campaigns, and funds are being raised often through shady deals which come to vitiate the process of governance. The poor quality of political finance and the power of money in the US political system are aptly summarised in Box 6.1,

Box 6.1. The Money Culture

The following quotes from Elizabeth Drew show amply how money culture is damaging democracy in the USA.

> The culture of money dominates Washington as never before; money now rivals or even exceeds power as the preeminent goal. It affects the issues raised and their outcome, it has changed employment patterns in Washington; it has transformed politics; and it has subverted values. It has led good people to do things that are morally questionable, if not reprehensible. It has cut a deep gash, if not inflicted a mortal wound, in the concept of public service....

> Washington has become a place where people come or remain in order to benefit financially from their government service....

> In 1998, according to the requirements of the Lobbying Disclosure Act of 1995, there were close to 11,500 lobbyists wandering the halls of Congress. However, this number isn't inclusive. A lot of people say they don't lobby—but they do something that seems a lot like it....

> More than ever, corporations or other interests that want to influence the Congress hire former Members of Congress or their aides as lobbyists, in order to ingratiate themselves with the current members. The former members have distinct advantages: they can go on the floor of the House or Senate and use their chambers' official dining rooms; even better, former House members can use the House gym, where a lot of business gets done.

Source: Excerpts by Elizabeth Drew (1999).

which presents excerpts from a book on the subject by eminent American journalist Elizabeth Drew. Situation in the USA with regard to power of money in Washington has worsened since Ms Drew's book. In particular, the decision of the Supreme Court on 21 January 2012, allowing companies to spend unlimited money in politics, has opened the floodgates for money in politics in the USA. Even the then President, Barack Obama, expressed his apprehensions:

> The supreme court has given a green light to a new stampede of special interest money into our politics. It is a major victory for big oil, Wall Street bankers, health insurance companies and other interests that marshal their power every day in Washington and drown out the voices of everyday Americans.[1]

It is unfortunate that some recent announcements suggest an open field for private contributions to political parties. In the original Company Act, there was a cap on political funding of 7.5 per cent of net profit of the company and the board resolution through which the funding that was to be done would reflect the name of the beneficiary political party. It appears that the government is proposing to do away with the cap and the name of the party that the company will fund will not have to be disclosed. If this indeed becomes a law, this alone will ensure that Bharat remains corruption-ridden and all the dreams of a corruption-*mukt* Bharat will remain dreams.

Fortunately, there are examples around the world of much cleaner political process than what obtains in the USA and now in India. Many countries in Europe such as Germany and Nordic countries provide better alternatives, though of course there is no one-size-fits-all solution and we should devise our own system.

---

[1] See http://www.deccanherald.com/content/52893/bigger-role-big-money-us.html (accessed on 3 May 2017).

European Guidelines on Political Finance[2]

'Financing Political Parties and Election Campaigns—Guidelines', prepared by the Council of Europe's integrated project 'Making Democratic Institutions Work', examines the advantages and disadvantages of different options for applying the organisation's standards, without prescribing an ideal model (see Box 6.2 for the main guidelines in this document).

According to these guidelines,

> The rules on financing political parties and on electoral campaigns must be based on the following principles: A reasonable balance between public and private funding, fair criteria for the distribution of state contributions to parties, strict rules concerning private donations, a threshold on parties' expenditure linked to election campaigns, complete transparency of accounts, the establishment of an independent audit authority and meaningful sanctions for parties and candidates who violate the rules.

In the past, there has been in legal and constitutional terms a somewhat negative attitude towards political parties which have long been seen as adverse to the general interest or as overriding the interest of the individual. Much of this changed in post-war period. In the Federal Republic of Germany, for example, the key role of political parties became acknowledged also in constitutional terms.

In considering the relevance of European experience, a starting point may be the constitutional provision for political parties. As noted in Legal Council's brief on electoral reforms in India, consideration may be given for constitutional amendment that

---

[2] Ingrid van Biezen (2003).

Box 6.2. European Guidelines on Political Finance

1. Parties in contemporary democracies need appropriate funding in order to carry out their core activities.

2. The structures of legal frameworks should be unambiguous, understandable, and transparent. They should address all components of the system of party and candidate financing necessary to ensure democratic participation and competition between parties.

3. Political parties and candidates should be partly financed through private means. Private sources of funding may be internal or external to the party.

4. States should consider introducing rules which limit the value of donations to political parties and candidates.

5. States should consider the introduction of rules which define or set limits on the acceptable sources of donations to political parties and candidates.

6. The legal framework of party financing should specifically limit, prohibit or otherwise regulate contributions from foreign donors.

7. State legislation may adopt special provisions for financing the electoral campaigns of political parties and candidates.

8. The state should consider adopting measures to prevent excessive funding requirements of political parties and candidates, such as establishing limits on expenditure for electoral campaigns.

9. The state should provide support to political parties and candidates in order to prevent dependence on private financial donors and guarantee equality of chances. State support may be financial.

10. The state may contribute—directly or indirectly—to the operational cost of party activity, election campaigns and the functioning of parliamentary party groups.

11. Political parties may receive indirect support from the state.

12. Objective, fair, and reasonable criteria should be applied regarding the distribution of state support. The state should enable new parties to enter the political arena and compete under fair conditions with more well-established parties.

13. State support should be limited to reasonable contributions. The state should ensure that any support from the state and/or citizens does not interfere with the independence of political parties and candidates.

14. The legal framework for party and candidate financing should include provisions for disclosure, reporting, monitoring, and enforcement.

15. The legal framework for party and candidate financing should include provisions for disclosure of sources of income and of expenditure.

16. States should require the accounts of political parties and of candidates to specify all donations received by the party, including the nature and value of each donation. Accounts should be made public, at least in summary form.

17. Rules concerning donations to political parties should also apply to all levels of the party organization and to all entities which are related, directly or indirectly, to a political party or are otherwise under its control.

18. States should require political parties and candidates to make their full accounts publicly available at regular intervals. At the very least, parties and candidates should present a summary of their accounts, including records of donations and expenditure.

19. States should provide for independent monitoring of the funding of political parties and electoral campaigns. Political parties and candidates should be required to present regular accounts to an independent authority.

20. States should require that any infringement of rules concerning the funding of political parties and election campaigns be subject to effective, proportionate and dissuasive sanctions.

recognises the constitutional position of political parties and calls upon the State to make provisions for its appropriate functioning.

A Proposal for Election Grants Commission (EGC)

Based upon review of the proposals on funding of elections, we propose a mechanism that can be regarded as a sort of public–private partnership for funding of elections and political parties.

It is proposed that an EGC be set up under the Election Commission to provide funding to political parties and election campaign of individual contenders under the state supervision and support. The funding will be done not in kind but in cash, thus avoiding the route of providing subsidies in kind which introduce distortions in the system. EGC will have a system for annual grants (through a system of matching the contributions made by individuals) to recognised parties and of election funding at central, state and local levels at the time of election, subject to a specified maximum support that can come from the state. As is done for charities such as United Way in the USA, private contributions (made by cheques or cash through postal money orders) can be channelled through EGC by a system of donor, designating the intended recipient, a specified political party or individual candidate. In all cases, EGC will specify a minimum and maximum of contributions to be received by the parties, including to individual candidates. The minimum specified will act as an eligibility criterion for matching grant by EGC. Unless this minimum is contributed by individuals, there will be no matching grants by EGC. For contributions at and above the minimum, EGC will make matching contributions until the total contributions (including the matching grants) received by party or individual candidate reach the specified maximum. EGC will also specify other eligibility criteria for the parties and candidates. For parties, this may involve compliance with rules about intra-party democracy, publication of audited accounts, etc. For individual candidates, this would involve criteria regarding criminal records, statement of assets and income and statement of expenses on elections. With one centralised institution for channelling political finance, it would be possible to ensure a full monitoring of such finance. The law can clarify that election results can be nullified at any time during the tenure of the representative, if the court finds that funding from illegal sources has been used in the election on a significant scale.

Will this involve undue burden on the state exchequer? Not according to the numbers available on reported cost of elections. It is estimated that in 2009 Lok Sabha elections, the amount of money spent by the government and the parties was about ₹10,000 crore. Assuming that similar expenditures may be made for state and local elections, the total cost of elections at three levels is ₹30,000 crore. Further assuming that given the uncertainties of electoral politics, an election once in three years can be allowed for, the 'annual' expenditures come out to be ₹10,000 crore. Even if we assume that by 2017, the election expenditures have trebled, they amount to ₹30,000 crore per year which is only about 0.20 per cent of GDP. If the state assumes half of the expenditures made by private funding, the total state expenditures may amount to be about 0.1 per cent of GDP which is quite modest in relation to other major expenditure items and subsidies. If state funding of political finance to this extent helps to make elections cleaner, it would be a worthwhile expenditure.

Rehabilitating the Badly Damaged Moral Compass by Grounding It in Spirituality

While formal and informal rules of behaviour are essential for proper functioning of society, they are by no means sufficient. An individual will often be in situations where the material gains from violations of codes of conduct will be higher than the expected value of costs from being caught in unlawful act and being punished for it. Even for social codes of conduct, the individual may well envisage escape from social detection and social punishment. Thus, unless there is a judge and jury within the self, chances of detection and punishment may not be enough to deter deviant behaviour. Following Gandhi, we need to say, 'The only tyrant I accept in this world is the still voice within'.

Unfortunately, however, performance of Gandhi's India in this crucial area is deplorable. People in power, whether in government or business or other areas, seem to be wallowing a corruption and comfort and complacency, succumbing to the seductions of corruption. One hears from so many learned quarters that corruption has entered into our bones. The corrupt feel no shame nor any fear. This is in sad contrast with many better functioning societies (e.g., in Nordic countries) where people take the rules of the system as their own and feel ashamed if found violating them. In India, how can we change the mentality? Only a moral compass implemented in the hearts of people concerned could possibly provide some antidote.

What could be the foundation for moral compass that we need? Some traditional religions tried to implant this compass through the fear of the all-seeing God and punishment after life. However, the era of the Enlightenment with primacy given to reason and verification dealt to a blow to that foundation for individual moral compass. With doubts about existence of God and after life, moral compass lost its foundation. At the same time, it was realised that without some moral values, societies cannot function well. Adam Smith, often seen as the architect of free market economy, was deeply concerned about malfunctioning of the market economy in the absence of moral philosophy, of which he was a distinguished professor. The philosophers in the West have been struggling hard to find some foundations for moral compass within a framework of rationality and without recourse to transcendental God. These efforts to implant moral compass in the human mind were thwarted by the Western notions of human mind being steeped in sin and religion being a matter of faith, rather than reason. In the wake of limited and convoluted progress of Western philosophies in finding a secure anchor of morality, there are recent signs in the West of revivalism in old-fashioned God and religious fundamentalism for providing a stronger anchor for a moral compass.

In India, we could have a better alternative in the philosophies developed, among others, by Aurobindo Ghosh, Swami Vivekananda and Mahatma Gandhi.

Drawing upon the Indian Vedantic tradition of the essentially divine nature of human being, Aurobindo developed the theory of spiritual evolution according to which evolution is essentially about evolution of consciousness. This gives a meaning and purpose to life. The purpose of life is the manifestation and development of divinity inherent in mankind. And what matters is development of consciousness in not just one individual but in all living beings. Development in one at the cost of development in others does not add to the sum total of consciousness and thus does not fulfil the purpose of evolution. All individuals, who at deep levels are partners in spiritual evolution, will find fulfilment only if they are contributing to the increase in the totality of higher consciousness through their own advance as well as assisting others' advance. And for appreciating the value of this contribution, there is no need for external agents, either governmental or social, to monitor individual performance. The moral compass is planted solidly in the individual through the concept of the divine self.

Swami Vivekananda elaborated on the concept of man as potentially divine and firmly rejected the notion of man as sinners. But he was also a man of action. He constantly called upon his fellow compatriots for social action for emancipation of women, for uplift of masses, for succour to the poor and deprived and set up institutions to promote these causes. These actions, in his view, were the best way to serve God and, one can say, to link up with Aurobindo's philosophy, to hasten the process evolution towards the manifestation of the divinity already in mankind. In all these teachings, he drew upon India's ancient traditions of Vedanta and Upanishads which touch deep chords in Indian minds, but he also constantly emphasised the underlying unity of all religions. Based upon his own experience and the practices of his guru Shri Ramakrishna that encompassed all the major religions of humanity, Swami Vivekananda developed a universalistic spiritual philosophy which passes the strictest test of secularism. In an India that was weak and fearful, he constantly called for strength and fearlessness. His words may well act as a tonic for India, which is in dire need for rebuilding its moral compass as well as social capital. Most of the vital issues for the transformation of our value system that we need today (e.g., developing identification with the masses and with the nation, warning against blind copying of the West, on national self-help, on chastising the upper classes, on liberation from oppression of the elites, on the importance of education for the masses, on quality of education, on attitude towards women, on the importance of ethical and spiritual culture for social progress, on avoiding pessimism, on freedom on the need for going beyond narrow nationalism, and on the role of India in the world) are like clarion calls providing all the inspiration we need.

Gandhi's unique contribution was to bring morality in politics and bring masses into political movement. Today, faced with institutional decay and widespread poverty and deprivation, the present leadership must transfer Gandhi's basic approach from the struggle for political freedom to the struggle for economic freedom. Prime Minister Modi must energise the masses about economic transformation and do so with a moral compass firmly implanted in our hearts. Just as Gandhi gave a religious overtone to the freedom struggle, he must make development a religious duty of everybody with zero tolerance for corruption. The Prime Minister has the potential of assuming the role of Raj Rishi as Rajiv Kumar (2015) puts it in his book *Modi and His Challenges*. In that role, he can persuade the country by example of having a strong moral compass in our dealings.

Freedom from corruption, vital though it is, is only an intermediate objective. A Swachh Bharat will, in the Prime Minister's vision, provide foundation for a Samriddha Bharat where there is prosperity for all and India regains its rightful place in the comity of nations. It is to these longer term issues that we turn now.

Making India Number One Again

Building on the foundations of a corruption-mukt Bharat, India can launch a program of transformation which will make it a developed country by 2050. It will become the largest economy in the world and global guru for socially, economically, ecologically and spiritually healthy prosperity.

Vision 2050

In his interview with Raj Chengappa published in *India Today* January 2017, Prime Minister Modi said:

> I believe India is standing at a watershed moment, on the cusp of actualizing its inherent potential as a developed nation and global leader....An India that is Swachh from all forms of filth.... I am... putting my heart and soul into building an enabling environment to spark a revolution that transforms India into a developed nation within one generation. I am confident the country can, and will.

These are inspiring words and should be taken seriously. I do not know if any other earlier prime minister of India has put forth such a vision with such force. It appeals to me particularly because on my return to India in 2005, I was inspired by the same vision and I spent about eight years writing a 400-page book (*India 2050*) elaborating how in my opinion we can do it. The book was published in 2014 and since then there have been developments that reinforce my optimism as well as developments that call for greater caution. The good news is of course the rise of Narendra Modi to power and the widespread support that the nation continues to show for him. The bad news is the deteriorating external environment which threatens to disturb the international order of trade, investment, mobility and peace in which several East Asian countries were achieving the goal of prosperity within one generation.

In the new environment, India must wake up to the hard realities and the grave risks it is facing. The USA is turning protectionist and that may have adverse consequences for our growth and security. The Islamic world, partly due to the policies in the West, is getting more and more angry and aggressive and that may have adverse consequences for our peace, both internal and external. China is in a triumphal mood and is eager to be dominant power certainly in the region and perhaps in the world. In this situation, what Deng Xiaoping said for China in the 1970s ('If we remain weak, we shall be bullied') applies to India today. If we remain weak and divided and dishonest, we will fall victim to external threats as we did in history many times before. The form may be different from what it was in the past, but our sovereignty (*azadi*) itself will be at stake.

That we must not let happen and the only way is that we get united and march together in concert to the goal of Swachh and Samriddha Bharat. In that task, we must rely largely on ourselves, our spiritual, intellectual, entrepreneurial and natural resources and overcome our colonial hangovers.

The demonetisation exercise has been revealing in many ways. It was a major initiative which came from a swadeshi mindset and could never have come from colonial-era textbooks. Those suffering from colonial hangover did their best to run it down and create confusion among the public. Their flailing efforts at discrediting Modi government only exposed the emptiness of Western-oriented intellectuals. Fortunately, the public with their swadeshi instinct understood its purpose well and showed solid support.

The leadership with swadeshi instinct also showed its steely determination and stood solidly behind its policies despite loud calls for rollback. And we are coming out of the episode well, though it could have been implemented with less pain. Moreover, it is clear that this is only a beginning. The pollution that has accumulated over centuries in our way of life will need long and sustained efforts for the clean-up. For charting the path forward, we must study our economic, social and political realities closely and come up with our own solutions. Colonial-era values and institutions will need a thorough overhaul. And in that gigantic task, we must give full support to inspired leadership that destiny has sent our way. At the same time, the leadership must improve implementation through better teamwork, the Gandhian way. The Gandhian way consists of taking a wide variety of people with different abilities, different attitudes and different backgrounds, bringing out the best in them and putting them to use in a common cause under clear guidance. The demonetisation exercise should be taken as an object lesson in how, despite good intentions, mistakes can be made due to inadequate teamwork. But it should also be a spur to fulfil the dream that the Prime Minister has put forward.

By 2050, India would have the largest population in the world. If India can indeed become a developed country by 2050, it would also be the largest economy in the world. If the *maha yagna* (great offering to fire) started by the present prime minister is continued, it would also be the cleanest spiritually and ecologically and a role model for the world. The space of Global Hegemon that was occupied by the USA is being vacated. China is trying to occupy that but it will fail to do so because of its democratic and spiritual deficit. That will be India's opportunity to fill that space not as a Hegemon but as a Guru: for fulfilment of the country and welfare of the world.

I present further the outcome of my studies and reflections over a 50-year period on how to make India regain its glory in the form of a 10-point programme for making India #1 again.

Quantify the Economic Dimension of India's 'Tryst with Destiny'

India is richly endowed with natural and human resources, particularly intellectual, entrepreneurial and spiritual capital. For much of the recorded history of the world, India has been the largest economy in the world. As noted by the eminent economic historian, Angus Maddison, in year 1, India accounted for 32.9 per cent of the global economy (as against China's 26.1%). This dominance continued for another 1,000 years and in year 1000, India's share was 28.9 per cent (as against China's 22.7%). With beginning of rule by externally oriented forces, this share began to decline: it was 16 per cent by 1820 (with China's 32.9%) and 4.2 per cent by 1950 (China's 4.6%). It barely increased to 5.4 per cent in 2001 after 50 years of Independence with externally oriented elitist rule.

This must change. We must realise our potential. To build on Prime Minister Nehru's famous Independence speech, we must redeem our tryst with destiny in economic dimension. Our natural and human resources are as good as those of any in the developed world and there is no good reason why our income should be any lower. Our long-term goal must be to catch up with per capita income of the developed countries which with our largest population will make us the largest economy once again. With high per capita income, we should also have high human development as all the high-income countries have today. We should have eliminated absolute poverty and provided health and education benefits to all, similar to what the most high-income countries have today. This is what our people demand and what our resources should deliver. Thus, catching up with high-income countries can become a defining goal of our long-term planning. Poverty eradication will remain important but it will be a by-product of shared prosperity.

Thus, we define a simple, clear and all-important goal: India's per capita GDP in 2005 PPP$ which was about $3,000 in 2010 must increase to about $33,000, an 11-fold increase. This will mean translation of the goal of 'sabka vikas' in numbers on income. . With some 25 per cent increase in population expected over the next few decades, this means an increase in GDP about 14-fold.

We should stop denigrating GDP. With all its shortcomings, this is the best summary statement of prosperity available and with high income, much else in human development follows, without exception.

Recognise that Our Initial Conditions are Difficult and We are in a Marathon Race Not a Sprint for Realising Our Goal

Given our abysmally low level of income today, achieving high income (or sabka vikas) will take time. In our calculation, the earliest we can achieve it is by 2050 when we celebrate the centenary of our republic. This will require sustained GDP growth at about 7 per cent per year over nearly 40 years. This is a marathon race, not a sprint. We need the mentality of a marathon runner: think ahead, be aware of hurdles, conserve strength, have patience and persevere. Do not go for quick bursts of growth based on cheap credit or fast exploitation of natural resources. Start preparing for building up human resources where gestation lag could be as much as a generation. Avoid getting into building structures which will last several generations and once built today will put constraints on future generations. Reforms needed for transformation will require changes in social attitudes and institutions which change only slowly over generations. The policies must have some basic constancy over a long time and the public must give the political leaders a long-term mandate for reforms.

In designing our road map, we must recognise that the circumstances of our growth programme are very different from those for pre-decessors of high-income stories. The West achieved high income through slow growth over two centuries with easy access to fossil fuels. East Asia achieved high-income status in a much shorter time but still with easy access to high carbon fossil fuel. India's growth story is starting when the fears of climate change are a dominant theme and we just cannot expect access to fossil fuel along the lines that our predecessors on high growth had. We must design a road map of growth which is low carbon in consumption and production.

First, it so happens that we seem to have some comparative advantage in knowledge business which is a low carbon activity. We have a youthful population which is the seedbed for knowl-edge development and which is hungry for betterment. India's democratic polity, its tradition of argumentation, its tradition of respect for knowledge, its low cost of production of human capital, its links with professionally inclined diaspora, its knowl-edge of English and its openness to the rest of the world, all these give India a special advantage in this area, especially compared with its chief competitor, China.

Second, it also so happens that India's growth programme is taking place when the Internet is revolutionising modes of trade, trans-port and communication when the earlier high-carbon modes are being replaced by low-carbon modes. The factor price equalisation theorem of trade is working with much greater force for those who can take advantage of trade through the Internet. India has got a head start in this area and it is clearly its area of future excellence.

Third, it so happens that because of our cultural traditions, most Indians prefer 'behind-the-desk' jobs to jobs on factory floor. That makes trade in knowledge activities a preferred job for Indians.

Altogether, India is ideally placed to be global capital of knowledge industry, a sort of 'Global Gurukul'.

This ground reality of India is very different from that of the West and of East Asia. This means that main sources of growth in India will be different from those of its predecessors: not manufacturing, but knowledge-intensive activities. Agriculture, mining and manufacturing will remain important. But they will not provide the main driving force. India's new temples will be neither dams, nor smoke-pouring factories nor gleaming six-lane highways. They will be schools, colleges, IT offices, hospitals and health clinics. Ministries of Human Resource Development (HRD) and Health will be the most important among the ministries for growth and development!

When we translate this theme into numbers, the growth pattern that emerges is basically different from the typical patterns that were obtained in earlier cases of development in the West or East Asia (see Table 7.1). Our obsession with manufacturing is overdone and our potential in HRD is vastly underutilised.

Table 7.1. Sectoral GDP Growth Rates (Annual %) in our Perspective Plan 2011–50

	2011–20	2021–30	2031–40	2041–50	2011–50
Education and research	11.2	9.5	6.7	4.3	7.9
Medical and health	10.2	12.0	11.7	11.7	11.0
Business services	11.0	11.4	8.0	5.3	8.9
Construction	9.3	10.4	6.1	2.3	7.0
Agriculture, forestry and fishing	3.4	3.0	2.0	1.1	2.4
Mining and quarrying	3.7	4.9	4.0	3.1	3.9
Manufacturing	7.0	7.8	5.4	3.4	5.9
Public administration, defence, and quasi-government bodies	7.3	7.7	5.6	4.0	6.2
GDP	7.3	8.3	6.2	4.3	6.5

Source: Ramgopal Agarwala (2014).

As noted in Table 7.1, main drivers of growth in short, medium and long terms will be HRD, business services and construction. This is where there is excess demand and massive growth potential. The performance of goods-producing sectors will be modest. Manufacturing will struggle to keep its share of GDP. There is hardly any area of sustained excess demand in the manufacturing sub-sectors, now or in the near future. The era when excess demand for things like cement or cars or scooters dominated Indian scene has been replaced by the era when excess demand for education, health and business services stares in the face. Investment should go where there is excess demand not where there is excess supply.

A road map to prosperity based on ground realities will be very different from the current rhetoric about programmes such as 'Make in India' focused on manufacturing-led growth. We should stop wasting time, energy and resources in old outmoded sectors and foster sectors where India's future lies. In trade liberalisation negotiations, we should focus on trade in services, particularly those that are facilitated by ICT.

Achieve Massive Expansion in HRD, Overcome Colonial Hangover in the Sector and Make It Value-based, Inclusive and Business-oriented

If capitalising on our human resources becomes our strategic thrust, we need a massive expansion in the sector. We need to match the human capital content of our labour force with that of the high-income countries by 2050. In fact, the human capital content of our labour force may have to be higher than that of developed countries, because we envisage substantial exports in knowledge sector. The Right to Education Act (RTE Act) must be effectively implemented by 2020. Universal access to pre-primary and higher secondary with a strong component of vocational education should be achieved latest by 2025. Gross enrolment ratio in higher education must be increased to some 70 per cent by 2030 to match that of the high-income countries today. R&D must be increased to some 2 per cent of GDP by 2030 and higher thereafter. Massive expansion in teacher training facilities would be essential and must be planned in advance. A perspective plan needs to work out the details of what is needed in terms of enrolment, soft and hard infrastructure and cost involved.

There are several characteristics of human capital formation that call for long-term planning. First, while gestation lag in physical capital formation is generally 3–5 years, the gestation lag in human capital formation is about 20 years from pre-primary education at the age of 3 to doctoral training by the age of 23 or so. If we want a high-quality scientist in 2040, we need to start training him in 2020. If the early training is of poor quality, it is very difficult to make up for it in later years. Thus, for realising our vision of high-income country by 2050, we must start ensuring that our early education system is in good shape without loss of time. A perspective plan should assess investment needs in education, taking into account the 20-year gestation lag.

Second, while ownership of physical capital can be concentrated in a few hands, human capital ownership has to be dispersed. The overall development of human capital can be achieved only if it is inclusive: no fertile mind can be left behind undeveloped, irrespective of gender, class, caste or religion. The access to education at all levels has to be made equitable for all and perhaps free and universal as is the case in high-performing countries such as Germany and Nordic countries. A perspective plan should articulate a time path for making pre-primary, primary, second-ary (including vocational) and higher education free and universal, consistent with the needs of reaching high-income status by 2050 and the resources available.

Third, increasing incomes will be associated with massive changes in age composition and rural–urban distribution of population. Schools set up today in rural areas for pre-primary and primary education will increasingly face shortage of students and may even have to be closed down, as is happening already in certain parts of the country. A perspective plan should articulate these changes in educational needs of population in different parts of the country and design strategies to cope with these changes. For example, if students in primary schools are expected to decline, then school facilities may be created in a cluster of villages rather than individual villages.

Even more important than quantitative expansion is the qualitative changes needed in the sector. The problem is that despite some pockets of excellence, our education system is performing poorly by international standards and is still in Macaulay mode: it is basically designed to produce 'a class of persons, Indian in blood and colour, but English (now American) in taste, opinions, in morals, and in intellect'. Gandhi spoke passionately against the Indian education system under the British. Many other scholars have talked about basic changes in our education system. But as in many other areas, our strong colonial hangover prevents changes in real life even though we talk eloquently about them. Basically, even after 70 years of Independence, our textbooks, the teaching methods and administrative systems remain mostly copies of the West without much attention to the Indian roots and conditions. It also remains elitist with a small fraction of population getting into elite educational institutions which separates them from the masses. The system is antithetical to creativity, relevance and inclusiveness. Some basic changes are needed which will probably take several decades and that is the right subject of a perspective plan.

First, the education sector must be value-based. Right from the pre-primary stage, children must imbibe the ethos of patriotism, honesty, democracy, community feeling, secularism and ecological sustainability. If this looks like saffronisation of education, so be it because saffron is the colour of the sun rising in India.

Second, we must overcome the craze for English-medium schools. No developed country teaches its children in any language other than mother tongue. English will remain a side language as in many European countries. Quebec in Canada provides an excellent example of how to give education and conduct business in the native language while achieving fluency in English.

Third, education after the elementary stage must become oriented towards skill formation. Vocational training must become an important and valued part of secondary and even higher education. Increasingly, knowledge imparting institutions will become integrated with knowledge-product-selling companies.

Fourth, as a trade-oriented sector, our knowledge sector must become closely integrated with the world economy with globalisation as a key feature.

Fifth, our knowledge sector must fully exploit the potential of ICT for generation, dissemination and marketing of knowledge.

Sixth, considering the power of vested interests in the existing institutions, reform effort should concentrate on getting the new institutions right: the philosophy of focusing on reform at the margin so successfully practised by the Chinese.

Provide Jobs and Social Security for All

There is much euphoria in India about our young population and the resultant demographic dividend. This is a grossly misleading view. There are many countries with high population growth and youthful population which are not necessarily growing fast. Among examples are Bangladesh, Pakistan and most of sub-Saharan Africa.

Within India too, if youthful population delivered high growth, UP and Bihar would be roaring tiger economies. In fact, on present trends, we are facing a demographic nightmare. Labour force is growing at least a million every month. Many of them now have some education and they are no longer willing to be absorbed in low-productivity agriculture or informal sector. They are looking for formal sector jobs in urban areas. And with formal sector employment growing at less than 1 lakh per month, this is leading to massive unemployment of moderately educated (or miseducated) youth with high expectations—a recipe for social and political disaster!

A vital task that a perspective plan should do is to prepare a clear-sighted view of jobs required in the next few decades to meet the needs of the burgeoning youthful labour force and assess where the jobs could come from. Improved skill formation would be an important part of it. So will the reform of labour laws which will introduce flexibility in labour deployment. But will these be enough? According to our analysis, not quite. Accelerated growth must be an accompaniment of these other reforms.

Where will this job-creating growth come from? Currently, it is expected that accelerated growth in manufacturing will do the job. According to our analysis, this is a gross mistake. As analysed in earlier section, under our ground realities, growth in manufacturing will be modest and it will at best absorb 15–20 per cent of incremental labour force. The major part of labour absorption has to be done by the service sector including construction. A perspective plan should lay bare the prospects of job creation in different sectors and correctly assess the potential of different sectors in this task. In our analysis, rapid growth as envisaged in Table 7.1 combined with labour market reforms and skill formation will provide decent employment to the growing labour force.

However, jobs created in the future may not be like the typical formal sector jobs as currently seen. The old concept of job with formal contract, fixed hours, fixed work place and life-time employment (which was a product of industrial civilisation) is may be on the way out due to emergence of ICT era. Jobs are may be increasingly one-task contract, flexible hours, flexible work place, self-employment and constant churning of tasks with female labour force (with continued household responsibilities) playing a major role. Start-ups, entrepreneurship development programmes and family businesses will become increasingly important. A perspective plan should articulate the changing concept of employment, so that there is not undue frustration about slow growth of formal sector employment.

With changing employment structure, provision of social security in the form of unemployment benefits, health benefits and pensions would increasingly cease to be connected with jobs. That responsibility will have to be assumed by the state with contributions from individuals. The perspective plan should develop the institutional structures for such contributory social security, with the state playing a key role in supplementing the individual contributions and managing the system.

Liberate Financial Sector from Wall Street Culture and Make It an Instrument for Providing Finance for All Entrepreneurs, Big or Small, Private or Public

In the Western world, there is now an increasing concern about the adverse effects of speculative high finance as it prevails in Wall Street and its associates. It is widely suspected that this high finance has contributed to sharp increase in inequality and to increased instability in these economies. Indian Dalal Street has been modelled on Wall Street (including installation of a bull as in Wall Street). The performance of capital markets has been modest in terms of mobilisation of finance for new investment or mobilisation of household savings. The rest of the financial sector has mercifully avoided the contagion of the American finance and thus saved the country from financial instability, characterising American finance and its associates. But the sector has not played its role in including the masses in the banking system and inter-mediating finance from household to all investors, small or big. Moreover, with inadequate spread of banking habits, cash econ-omy has remained a substantial part of the system with 'black economy' now forming a high share of the economy.

If our vision of the economy is to be realised, all this must change. The economy will need about 40 per cent of GDP in investment by the state as well as private sector, big and small. Financial sector must be designed to help in mobilisation of these vast resources. Capital markets must develop a transparent and trustworthy system where savers with some appetite for risk taking can expect on average a decent rate of return on their savings higher than in FDs in banks or elsewhere. Banking must be made universal, assisted by ICT, so that most transactions become cashless which would also provide a check on growth of black economy. Banks must also develop their lending practices which can support start-ups and small entrepreneurs. The whole financial sector must also contribute to fiscal resource mobilisa-tion by introduction of selective FTT which would be a low-cost instrument of taxation and may allow reduction of other taxes (particularly income tax) which would improve compliance and reduce the menace of black money.

The perspective plan would lay out the investment require-ments for achieving the development targets and analyse various reforms in the financial sector needed to perform its job of financial intermediation.

Redefine 'Good Life' in Ecologically Sustainable and Spiritually Fulfilling Terms

In a sharp departure from our traditions and Gandhian principles, the dominant theme in Indian development is to replicate the American lifestyie. In the words of Jairam Ramesh, 'There is no doubt that India is following American consumption patterns. There is a single paradigm—one model and energy-intensive, private-transport-intensive model and economic growth'. Our analysis (presented in the book *India 2050*) shows that given our constraints of land, carbon space and water availability, it is simply not feasible for us to replicate the American lifestyle which also happens to be unhealthy and stressful, and thus not worth copying. We also argue that it is possible to have a different high-income low-carbon lifestyle (grounded in our traditions) which will be more fulfilling and feasible within our resource constraints.

The perspective plan should make a thorough analysis of the implications of global warming syndrome on our development prospects. Is it possible for us to replicate the American lifestyle? Is American lifestyle desirable? Is a high-income low-carbon lifestyle feasible? What are the contours of such a lifestyle and its associated production system? What are the instruments available to achieve the required transformation? How do we achieve the goal of clean air, clear water, clean rivers and abundant greenery?

India has an opportunity and the necessity of designing a low-carbon, ecological sustainable lifestyle that is satisfying for the rich nation and also giving happiness and fulfilment to its people. No country has done it so far, though there are pockets of such efforts in many countries. Having the advantage of being a late-comer, India can do it, and if it does, then it will be a pioneer. It will be ahead of China as well as the USA who will be struggling to achieve low-carbon economy, having grown fast on high-carbon production and consumption systems. This will be part of the programme of making India first, ahead of China.

Overcome Village Romanticism and Develop Knowledge-based Decentralised Cities

It is an iron law of economics without a single exception that as a country gets richer, the share of rural population declines and that of urban area increases. This in turn is due to two other iron laws: the share of consumption of agricultural products decreases as income increases and the productivity in agricultural sector does not increase as fast as it does in non-agricultural sector that operates mainly in urban areas. As India gets richer, urbanisation will increase and village population will shrink. There is no point in trying to push rural development artificially. Instead, we should try to develop small towns which will provide services to village clusters of 100 or so villages.

While urbanisation is essential, we do not have to follow the pattern developed in the age of industrialisation with megalopolis of tens of millions of people, carbon-intensive transport and habitation pattern. Many of these big cities have been built on coast areas which are now vulnerable to climate change. Instead, we should develop knowledge-centric cities as extension of each district capital. These will be new cities which can be developed on new principles of ecologically sound infrastructure and new social and economic policies.

According to our projections, between now and 2050, there will be some 800 million new urbanites, half of which can be accommodated in some 800 new district capital city extensions and the other half in some 8,000 new tehsil town extensions, providing services to some 100 villages each.

In this vision, we will not try to create competition among different towns and cities but, following the principle of 'sabka saath sabka vikas', help development of all towns and cities. Such development will be largely self-help based with support provided by central and state governments as needed. This will create an atmosphere of enthusiasm about development of all in the country, making it a mass movement for development.

Land will be acquired by the state authorities for this purpose with compensation given on the basis of a decent multiple of the present value of income streams originating from the land along with employment guarantee for all those who are affected by land acquisition. The conversion of land for city/town will create windfall in the value of land which will accrue to the state authorities and will be utilised for development of infrastructure of these cities and towns. This will make financing for development of these new towns and cities manageable.

The above vision of urban development would have important implications for planning process. At present, the NITI Aayog is supposed to start with village plans and aggregate them into national plan. This is simply not feasible. It will be years before six lakhs of villages can prepare their plans and they would be of such different qualities as to defy aggregation. The alternative along the lines of Chinese practice would be as follows. The perspective plan will prepare the broad contours of development at national level as discussed in this chapter. The state authorities will take this into account and prepare a more detailed plan for the state. District authorities in turn will take into account the state plans and prepare an even more detailed plan for the district. The performance of the whole country will be taken into account by the central authority in preparing the next round of plan and the process will be repeated.

The perspective plan should work out the broad contours of urbanisation that will be associated with projected growth scenario at aggregate and sectoral levels. It should also delineate the principles of decentralised knowledge-based urban pattern.

DEMONETISATION: A MEANS TO AN END?

It should also specify the programme for strengthening planning capacity at the state and district levels for translating the broader guidelines into more specific projects and programmes.

Recognise the Role of State in Reforms for Transformation and Build Democratic Socialism Based on Our Constitution and Political Realities

There is much euphoria in India about the market-oriented reforms introduced in 1991. These reforms were introduced when the country was facing severe balance of payment problems and had no option but to follow the programme of liberalisation and marketisation that the West was pushing at that time. Fortunately, neither the prime minister nor the finance minister nor the political mainstream really believed in them and India got out of the tutelage of IMF and the West within two years. The so-called market reforms were followed but not with the haste and pressure to which other countries in sub-Saharan Africa and former Soviet Union were subjected. In the West, there is now a widespread disenchantment with the free market philosophy pushed in the 1980s and 1990s. It is widely agreed that these reforms in the West (particularly the USA and the UK) contributed a lot to increased inequality and instability in the system without adding to long-term growth trend. Search is now on for a better alternative to the free market era in the West. In India, the reform era has helped to accelerate growth rate, thus contributing heavily to poverty reduction. But it has also led to increased inequality and to increased vulnerability. More importantly, the growth rates that the regime has delivered are well below our potential and our needs for employment creation. We need a new paradigm, a new balance between market and the state that will enable us to reach our long-term goal.

As noted above, for reaching our long-term goal, we need heavy investment in physical and social infrastructure, provide access to education, health and social security to all and make consumption and production patterns ecologically sustainable. We need to encourage the private sector to contribute to this task as much as they can, and for that purpose we should improve ease of doing business and liberalise rules for foreign private investment. But the private sector now happens to be debt-distressed and risk averse. It cannot meet India's investment needs. The state has to play a lead role in building social and physical infrastructure and providing education, health and social security to all. This means discarding our old favourite Anglo-American market-oriented system in favour of social market economy model of Germany and Nordic countries. This will be quite different from the socialism of Nehru era which was characterised by deep distrust of profits, private sector and markets and a faith in the state to allocate total resources of the economy in whichever direction it wanted. But it will also be quite different from Reagan–Thatcher era which is characterised by a deep distrust of the state and blind faith in the equilibrating and optimising properties of the free market and private sector. In the proposed model, private sector will be a key player in producing goods and services which have low externalities. But the government will not be a dirty word and will play a key role where substantial externalities prevail as in HRD and ecological management. This may imply that over time, public sector may have to manage 40–50 per cent of GDP as is the case in Germany and Nordic countries. It could also be similar to what obtains in China under the rubric of socialism with Chinese characteristics. In Indian conditions, we can call it democratic Socialism with Gandhian characteristics, Gandhian in terms of being inclusive, ecologically sustainable, spiritually guided and rooted in the soil of the country.

This switch to democratic socialism may be not only economically necessary but also a constitutional and political imperative. We cannot ignore the fact that as of now our Constitution provides for a socialist republic. Pure capitalism will be unconstitutional. Equally important, in our socio-economic conditions, a large majority of voters have antipathy to business community. There are simply not enough votes for being business-friendly in India. Unless a political party wants to indulge in double-talk, it cannot be capitalism-oriented and win elections. Thus, in some ways, India is in a sweet spot similar to what the USA and the UK were in the post-war era: an inclusive HRD which is a political necessity is also an economic imperative.

The perspective plan should make a clear-sighted review of the relative role of state and private sector necessary for achieving our long-term goal. It should also make a detailed analysis of how the public sector will mobilise resources needed to fulfil its obligations in the envisaged scenario.

Mainstream Spirituality into Development and All Walks of Life, Public and Private

The above scenario will involve a vastly expanded role of the public sector. It will require enormous efforts to improve the quality of governance. The starting point for that will be administrative reforms on which erudite committee reports are available. In particular, implementation of the recommendations of the Second Administrative Reforms Commission will go a long way to improve the quality of administrative services. We will also need to reform the political finance so that election process is not dominated by money power. The menace of black money which promotes corruption has to be tackled. But we have to go beyond that and strengthen the moral compass which has become dangerously weakened not only in the public sector but also in the private sector. The social and political arguments for probity in public and private life popularised in the Enlightenment period in Europe do not provide strong enough antidote to amoral behaviour. It is the inner voice that has to be awakened and that is the sphere of spiritual forces which have been dangerously ignored in the so-called secular tradition popularised by the West.

In India, we must capitalise on Gandhi's insight and pull the spiritual string which is still quite strong in most Indian hearts. Development must be made our dharma, a religious duty to contribute to sabka vikas. Just as Gandhi gave a religious touch to every family contributing to swaraj through, among other things, charka, we must give a religious touch to every family contributing to economic swaraj through giving the best possible education to their children.

Recent discussions on climate change have shown that it is extremely difficult to overcome the vested interests in a business-as-usual scenario through secular arguments. The intervention of Pope Francis laying out a moral and spiritual case for managing climate change is widely seen as a powerful contribution. For India too, it would be desirable to mobilise the spiritual leaders to support the difficult case for changing values and lifestyles promoted by the West. Similarly for developing value-based education and for overcoming barriers of caste, class or religions and creating an inclusive society, the help of spiritual leaders need to be sought.

The perspective plan should review the subject as to how religious forces which have often created divisions and strife can be mobilised to make the case for inclusiveness and ecological sustainability.

Overcome Colonial Hangover and Develop a Neo-swadeshi Mindset which Learns from All but is Rooted in India's Culture

A tiny minority (perhaps 1–2%) of the population has been ruling India since Independence. Most of them suffer from deep colonial hangover. They are in thrall of the West and have low regard for India's past and low expectations about its future. They look at India's history and the present through Western narratives and are generally looking for validation (permission slips) for their actions from the West. They have continued the colonial mode in education system, administrative system, law, police, judiciary and much else. The vast majority of population who basically grow up with Indian ancient culture and traditions are diffident and sub-missive to the elite. The creativity of the elite is stifled because of their imitative mindset and of the masses due to their diffidence. The Indian situation is quite different from that of East Asia or Bangladesh or the West where even small countries have pride in their history and culture and grow from their roots. If India is to become a developed country, it must overcome its colonial hangover and develop its swadeshi mindset.

In the struggle for Independence, swadeshi was defined largely as forsaking the foreign goods and using domestic products. While some preference for domestic products is desirable, swadeshi in the new conditions has to be defined in broader terms as being rooted in our own history and culture but learning from the best anywhere, not just from the old colonial masters. In the immortal words of Gandhi:[1]

> I do not want my house to be walled in on all sides and my windows to be stuffed. I want the cultures of all lands to be blown about my house as freely as possible. But I refuse to be blown off my feet by any.

This philosophy can be called neo-swadeshi. The perspective plan should be an occasion to implement this philosophy. Under the perspective plan exercise, a thorough search will be made for success stories around the world and in India. The success stories in each area will be examined for their relevance in India and an

---

[1] http://www.great-quotes.com/quote/645446 (accessed 17 May 2017).

appropriate design developed. For example, in the field of education, Finland may be regarded as a success story to be studied. For combining English with local language in education and business life, Quebec may be a role model. In health care, Cuba seems to be a success story to consider in India's conditions. For social security, Singapore may be a role model to be considered. For balance between state and market, Germany and Nordic countries may be considered. For globalisation with full protection of domestic industries, Japan, South Korea and China may be the role models. For dietary patterns, India's vegetarianism may be a role model. For physical and mental exercise, Yoga systems may be the way to go. For state-supported finance for political parties and elections, many European countries (such as Denmark) may provide good role models. The basic point is liberation of mind from the colonial hangover and daring to think for ourselves.

Q&A on Demonetisation

Annexure I

1. On the Process of Demonetisation

Q.1: Was the timing for demonetisation right? Nowhere else such an action has been taken in a well-functioning economy. Why was it done in India when the economy was in a good shape?

A.1: Demonetisation in India was not a monetary exercise to take out excess money supply as was usually the case in demonetisation exercises elsewhere. The Indian exercise was motivated by a desire primarily to check corruption and black money. It was expected that there will be some initial costs of such an exercise. So, a relatively well-functioning economy was in fact a good context for the demonetisation exercise.

Q.2: Was demonetisation politically motivated?

A.2: Yes, but not for short-run political gains. For a major decision with potentially huge electoral consequences, political dimension is always a consideration for any government. However, in this case, it was not narrow political advantage to be gained by mopping up black money to be handed over to the electorate but the long-term political gain by meeting the public's deeply felt desire to do something about the chronic problem of corruption in the country. It was the virulent criticisms of the opposition parties that seemed to have been politically motivated and unfortunately for them it boomeranged on them as the electorate refused to buy their story.

Q.3: Was demonetisation an undemocratic/despotic act constituting a breach of trust?

A.3: No. Demonetisation was done according to the democratic rules by a duly elected government. There was nothing despotic about it and even the vocal opposition parties did not raise the issue. Nor did the public show any sign of loss of trust in the Indian currency. The accusations were merely academic.

Q.4: Was demonetisation in line with legal requirements?

A.4: Yes. The issue of legality was raised before the Supreme Court. After hearing both sides of the story and due deliberations, the Supreme Court refused to stay the demonetisation order, though it did urge the government to try and minimise the disruptions to the public.

Q.5: Was RBI given sufficient time to hold deliberations on demonetisation?

A.5: No. The governor of RBI has stated in front of the Parliamentary Committee and elsewhere that deliberations on demonetisation between the government and RBI had been going on for quite some time. These statements do not clarify if there were open-minded discussions or more of instructions from the government. Nor is it clear if the involvement was only of the governor or of the board. The general impression is that the government leadership was highly distrustful of its colleagues and partners in the government and RBI in the name of secrecy, and it failed to make adequate preparations for this momentous decision. It has been rightly pointed out that in connection with preparation of budget every year, scores of officials are involved without any problem on account of secrecy. A big decision like demonetisation should not have been restricted to a few selected officials, and RBI should have had due deliberations and made adequate preparations for the decision. The focus on secretiveness and suddenness was overdone and it did not achieve the objective of frustrating money laundering activities.

Q.6: Was autonomy of RBI compromised?

A.6: No. There was no compromise of the autonomy of RBI. According to RBI Act, RBI is not independent of the GOI and is supposed to work in line with the GOI. In any case, monetary policy is too serious a business to be left to unelected RBI officials. The monetary policy has to be coordinated with other dimensions of macroeconomic management and the elected officials of the GOI have to take responsibility for macroeconomic management which has big implications for the welfare of the people. Such a big decision as demonetisation which has had far-reaching implications could not possibly be left to decision-making or vetoing to the unelected officials of RBI. The emphasis on autonomy of central banks is a reflection of historical forces in the Anglo-American world and is not shared by high-performing economies of East Asia. Those in India who are obsessed with autonomy of RBI are suffering from colonial hangover and should learn from the demonetisation episode that such autonomy is not desirable in the Indian context. A monetary policy like defence policy has to be finally decided by elected officials with of course due inputs from the technical experts.

Q.7: Is there any other country which has restricted people's right to withdraw their own money from banks?

A.7: No. There is no such precedent. But there is always a first time. Some restrictions of withdrawals apply even now in the form of limits on withdrawal through ATMs. In fact, the possibility of such restrictions is a good precedent for preventing runs on banks and bank failures. The right to property is not being compromised.

Q.8: Would a gradual process of demonetisation have been better?

A.8: Yes. A gradual process of demonetisation would have caused less disruption without necessarily losing the benefits. The whole idea was to shorten the opportunity for money laundering by people holding unaccountable cash. But the 50-day period was good enough for most black money holders and most of the currency demonetised has been returned. Thus, to the extent the purpose of short period for deposit was to prevent money laundering, it has not been achieved. This should have been anticipated and a longer period allowed to minimise disruptions.

Q.9: Was introducing ₹2,000 notes logical?

A.9: No. The whole argument for demonetisation of high-value notes was that these high denominations facilitate black money circulation. Thus, to withdraw ₹1,000 notes and introduce ₹2,000 notes was not logical. Moreover, the issuance of ₹2,000 notes magnified the disruption because people withdrawing these notes were unable to use them in their normal transactions.

Q.10: Was there repeated change of rules indicator of mismanagement?

A.10: Yes. There was mismanagement of the process. In 50 days since 9 November, there were 65 notifications from RBI about the procedures for taking deposits, giving out cash, etc. On several occasions, there were changes within the same day. This caused great confusion among the public and put the whole process in disrepute. It is true that given the unprecedented nature of demonetisation in India, some surprises were inevitable and some changes in rules as the process unfolded were natural. However, the authorities should have expected money laundering efforts on large scale and designed procedures on the basis of detailed consultations with the experts. It is because of the inadequate consultations that precautions were not taken. Announcements of changes within one day were excessive and indicated misman-agement on procedures. It was truly a picture of a 'flailing state' hitting this way or that to check money laundering, an effort in which they largely failed. This should have been handled better.

Q.11: Was there an unfair change of goal posts?

A.11: No. The basic goals were unchanged. Some elaboration and refinements of objectives were perfectly legitimate.

The critics have argued that in his speech on 8 November, the Prime Minister did not once use the word 'cashless'. It was all about 'black money' (18 times) and fake currency (5 times). By 27 November, the Prime Minister shifted gears and in two speeches that day he mentioned 'cashless' 24 times and 'black money' only 9 times! In their view, this was an unfair change of goal posts.

The government was right in changing the emphasis of the exer-cise as it evolved. There is no good reason why the first thoughts must be the last thoughts in a complex exercise such as demon-etisation. The promotion of digital payment system (DPS) can be rightly regarded as an elaboration of how demonetisation would incentivise movement to a system where payments would leave a trail and thus reduce the risk of generation of black money.

Q.12: Was there monumental mismanagement in the process of demonetisation?

A.12: Yes and no. Yes, there was mismanagement but it was not monumental.

The critics have argued that there was not adequate supply of new notes. The new notes were slightly smaller than the old notes and ATMs were not set up to handle new notes. The queues at the ATMs and for exchanging and even depositing old notes were just too long and often ended in frustration. All this is true. The process should have been managed better. But given the mammoth character of the demonetisation exercise, some disruptions were expected. And the fact that the public took it in its strides goes to show that the mismanagement was not as monumental as the critics assert.

Q.13: Why was cooperative banking system which serves large number of people prevented from handling new currency and taking deposits?

A.13: Yes, it was a mistake not to allow the cooperative banks to participate in handling new notes. This shortfall was also due to the excessive haste with which demonetisation was done.

Q.14: Should government have been faster in replenishing with new money? Why were there not enough notes of ₹500?

A.14: Yes. The government should have printed enough ₹500 notes before going for demonetisation. The government rushed into action for the fear that rumours about demonetisation were spreading and a quick action was necessary, even without adequate supply of new notes. Actually, rushing did not prevent money laundering as could have been and was predicted. It only caused massive hardship. That the public took it on its chin is a tribute to the patience of the public, not an excuse for government's mismanagement.

Q.15: Was it a political masterstroke for reputation as anti-corruption crusader?

A.15: Yes, it worked out like that. Whether planned or not, the move was taken as a proof of the seriousness of the government about eradicating black money and corruption. Whatever be the costs and benefits in strict in economic terms, the public gave a resounding vote of confidence in the government and seemed prepared to give it a wider and longer mandate to finish the job.

Q.16: Is cashless mode costless? Does it infringe on privacy and freedom of choice?

A.16: No, cashless mode is not costless, but the gains are worth the cost. Yes, digital modes may infringe on privacy to some extent but that is the cost worth paying for greater transparency.

The case for digital payments does not mean cashless system, only less-cash system. For those who want to keep privacy of their purchases, cash payment will remain an option, though around the world payments on private items are made through DPS without much concern about privacy. The costs of switching to DPS are modest. Even these could be taken care of by government in view of the long-term merits of digital payments. In any case, even printing and distribution of cash costs something to RBI. If these costs are reduced through DPS even with some subsidy, net costs to the authorities may not be significant.

Q.17: Was there a less costly alternative to the same goals?

A.17: Yes. It could have been done with less disruption through a gradual process.

Critics have rightly argued that the decision could have been taken after adequate consultation and preparation for remonetisation through new notes. Only ₹1,000 notes might have been demonetised which would have meant deposits in the banks of a large proportion of high-denomination notes. Black money in ₹1,000 notes would have come out in the open to the same extent that it has. Switch to less-cash system through incentives could have been promoted without the misery of demonetisation.

Q.18: What are the different ways of laundering money that are being practised and were they anticipated or action taken to block these avenues? Could they provide means of catching the culprits and plugging future loopholes?

A.18: Yes, the channels of money laundering have been revealed and that could provide the basis for future action to plug these loopholes. Important among these are temple donations, agricultural incomes, shell companies, benami Jan Dhan accounts and fake political parties. Income tax laws should be modified to plug these holes.

II. On the Costs and Benefits of Demonetisation

Q.19: What are the transaction costs of demonetisation exercise? Will those be exceeded by transaction gains?

A.19: Transaction costs and gains of the demonetisation exercise cannot be estimated meaningfully. And in any case, a big public policy decision has to be evaluated in terms of national gains in socio-economic-political terms and not in narrow 'transactional' terms.

Some critics of demonetisation tried to estimate the transaction costs in terms of items such as foregone wages of those who have to stand in queues, costs of banks who could not do any other business, cost of printing and distributing new notes, loss of business in factories and markets. They estimated gains in terms of black money not returned and thus giving a windfall to the public sector. And they ended up declaring the exercise as a net loser in transaction terms.

The transactions approach is too limited for evaluation of costs and benefits of a major public policy action. The costs are more in terms of what it costs to the people in terms of loss of income and employment in the short and the long term. And benefits are in terms of reduced level of corruption, counterfeit currency, terrorist activity, etc., not just in terms of cash flow to the government/RBI. Those standing in queues may in fact be earning some money by doing money laundering. Banks may gain from extra deposits. Gains to the government may occur for greater formalisation of the informal sector and an enhanced tax base.

Q.20: Will a large amount of currency be extinguished and accrue to the RBI/government as a windfall?

A.20: Yes. It could have been a big windfall if a large amount of currency failed to return to the open system. However, it was found that there were many channels for money laundering at a small commission of 10–30 per cent. It is reported that most of the demonetised currency has come back to the system. In fact, there is speculation that with bank staff under pressure and unable to do checking for counterfeit currency, even some counterfeit money has been deposited. Thus, the money deposited may even exceed the money in circulation with a net loss to the system to the extent of counterfeit money accepted as deposits. RBI has not been publishing the figures of currency returned on the plea that review is going on to avoid double-counting. The speculation is that RBI may in fact be facing an embarrassing situation. Thus, the gains accruing to RBI/government through demonetisation may not be substantial.

Q.21: What is the cost of demonetisation in terms of growth in the short and long terms?

A.21: It is inherently difficult to estimate growth effects of demonetisation in the short or long term. The dismal effects of demonetisation on growth in the short term estimated by critics were based on weak analysis and did not happen. The longer run effects are also difficult to estimate. The assumption of supporters of demonetisation that it would deliver cleaner and faster growth are not based on any solid analysis and may not happen without some additional countervailing measures.

In the immediate aftermath of demonetisation, anecdotal stories of loss of income started pouring in from state after state and sector after sector. Analysts also raised the spectre of nose-dive of the economy and of recession. But they underestimated the resilience of the economy and the early results show only modest losses of income. But the story is not over yet. Final estimates for the year 2016–17 may yet contain surprises. And the longer run effects of curtailing black money and corruption on the economy through wealth effects and uncertainty effects may yet result in lowering growth rates unless the government takes measures to stimulate the economy.

Q.22: Will demonetisation have net positive or net negative effect on the banking system?

A.22: Despite the short-term stress, the demonetisation exercise will have net positive effect on the banking system.

Critics point out that the banking system has been under terrible stress during the demonetisation period. They are now saddled with huge deposits on which they have to pay interest. But these deposits are of uncertain duration and do not provide basis for any medium-term ending. If depositors cannot be confident of withdrawing their deposits when they need it, then there may increase reliance on cash. In any case, demand for credit is low and if they push for lending, they may end up with NPAs. They can deposit excess deposits with RBI and buy G-Secs. But the availability of G-Secs is uncertain. The banks may have to start charging for their services to their customers more than before and that may not be good for their business.

During the period of demonetisation, banks faced a tough task. But with some exceptions, they did a good job and public confidence in banking system and deposits is high. With gradual move to formalisation of the informal sector, increased use of DPS and greater transparency in real estate markets, banks' business and earnings will increase substantially. The episode of government putting limits on withdrawal for a temporary period may also have benefit for the banking system. Instead of worrying too much about capital adequacy as per Basle III rules, the banks can concentrate on improving the quality of their operations with the knowledge that there is little risk of run on the banks because the government has demonstrated its capacity to put limits on withdrawals under special circumstances. The banks are in fact lowering their interest rates and for some banks, their market valuations are improving.

Q.23: Will demonetisation contribute to curbing inflation?

A.23: Yes, it will. Black money is hot money with a high velocity of circulation. It has been going into real estate, luxury goods including jewellery, travel, health and even educational services and driving up their prices, thus contributing to general price inflation. To the extent that demonetisation curbs incidence of black money, it will curb the inflation rate in these areas and thus help in curbing inflation in general.

Q.24: Will demonetisation help in reducing interest rates?

A.24: Yes, it will. Deceleration of inflation in some important segments as noted above should help in reducing inflation rates. The banks are flush with funds and are looking for ways of increasing their lending. Some banks have already reduced their interest rates and more should follow. However, a lot depends on the macro-policy stance that the government takes. If it continues with the notion that a high interest rate policy helps in reducing inflation and that growth performance is good enough, then it may continue the high interest rate policy. If on the other hand, the government starts getting worried about demonetisation-induced slowdown, and moves to an expansionary monetary and fiscal policy, then interest rates may come down further.

Q.25: How will demonetisation affect flow of new black money?

A.25: Not much by itself but a lot with suitable supplementary measures.

Contrary to expectations, not many black market operators have lost sleep over demonetisation. They have found ways of money laundering. In fact, old habits die hard. The attractions of evading taxes and the government scrutiny of businesses are indeed high, and black economy had become a way of life in India. There are indeed signs of its re-emergence after demonetisation. There are anecdotal stories of doctors again asking for their fees in cash and retailers highlighting to the buyers the savings through cash payments. A whole slew of measures are necessary to change the way of life of black economy and the government should recognise the enormity of the problem and design measures for the cure. Among these measures would be big push for digital payments, formalisation of informal sector, drastic reform of direct taxes and quality of tax administration.

Q.26: Is there a risk of re-emergence of inspector raj and its associated harassment and corruption?

A.26: Yes, there is. The government needs to deal with this problem with great care and wisdom.

The government is clearly surprised and angry to see how widespread money laundering has been, and very little of demonetised currency has failed to return to the system. Now the government's boast is that all that black money is in the open and by suitable taxation and persecution, it will show the money launderers who has the last laugh. In this mood, the government may well unleash a grievous form of inspector raj. Already lakhs of notices have gone out asking for explanations for cash deposits above a certain amount. This may cause much harassment to the public without necessarily satisfactory outcome for the government. At the operational level, the money launderers will be familiar with the low-level contact officers who will be open to compromise. Now that remonetisation is making progress, money launderers will be able to withdraw cash and make deals with grass-roots revenue officers. Even in cases where persecution will be initiated, money launderers will be able to use the slow court system to delay and even deny justice.

The task of identifying the launderers is huge, and the government should not underestimate its magnitude and complexity. It needs a multi-pronged programme involving reforms of tax system, bureaucracy, judiciary and police. No quick results should be expected.

Q.27: Will the real estate sector benefit from demonetisation?

A.27: Yes and no. Yes, it will benefit the real estate buyers who were priced out of market due to high and rapidly increasing housing prices fed by black money. But it will hurt those who became rich overnight due to boom in land and housing prices fed by black money. The old situation was unnatural. Demonetisation-induced correction in the real estate market will be healthy.

Q.28: Will demonetisation reduce the incidence of black money with political parties?

A.28: Not by demonetisation alone and not by the recent signs of government policy.

Under the current system, political parties do not need to show the sources for contributions below ₹20,000. During the demonetisation exercise, there is no evidence of any political party failing to launder their cash. For the future, the government is trying to set up a new system of funding through bonds. Under this system, the individuals and companies can buy bonds from RBI in their names through white money but then contribute to political parties anonymously. Thus, the needs for using white money and for maintaining anonymity will both be met.

Actually, the proposed scheme is toothless. Any individual can buy the bonds from its recorded income while meeting its expenses in cash from income (as is done extensively by many companies specialising in money laundering). Businesses and corporations can easily find individuals doing this job for a commission. Thus, political funding remains an area for full play of black money with all its deleterious effects on the society. More creative thinking is necessary in this area and it is not clear if the government has the political will for tackling this tough task.

The Speech of Prime Minister Modi on 8 November 2016 on Demonetisation

My dear citizens,

I hope you ended the festive season of Diwali with joy and new hope. Today, I will be speaking to you about some critical issues and important decisions. Today, I want to make a special request to all of you. You may recall the economic situation in May 2014 when you entrusted us with an onerous responsibility. In the context of BRICS, it was being said that the 'I' in BRICS was shaky. Since then, we had two years of severe drought. Yet, in the last two and a half years, with the support of 125 crore Indians, India has become the 'bright spot' in the global economy. It is not just we who are saying this, it is being stated by the International Monetary Fund and the World Bank.

In this effort for development, our motto has been 'Sab Ka Saath Sab Ka Vikas': We are with all citizens and for development of all citizens. This government is dedicated to the poor. It will remain dedicated to them. In our fight against poverty, our main thrust has been to empower the poor and make them active participants in the benefits of economic progress.

The Pradhan Mantri Jan Dhan Yojana,

the Jan Suraksha Yojana,

the Pradhan Mantri Mudra Yojana for small enterprises,

the Stand-up India programme for Dalits, Adivasis and Women,

DEMONETISATION: A MEANS TO AN END?

the Pradhan Mantri Ujjwala Scheme for gas connections in the homes of the poor,

the Pradhan Mantri Fasal Beema Yojana and Pradhan Mantri Krishi Sinchai Yojana to protect the income of farmers,

the Soil Health Card Scheme to ensure the best possible yield from farmers' fields and

the e-NAM National Market Place scheme to ensure farmers get the right price for their produce—these are all reflections of this approach.

In the past decades, the spectre of corruption and black money has grown. It has weakened the effort to remove poverty. On the one hand, we are now No. 1 in the rate of economic growth. But on the other hand, we were ranked close to 100 in the global corruption perceptions ranking two years back. In spite of many steps taken, we have only been able to reach a ranking of 76 now. Of course, there is improvement. This shows the extent to which corruption and black money have spread their tentacles.

The evil of corruption has been spread by certain sections of society for their selfish interest. They have ignored the poor and cornered benefits. Some people have misused their office for personal gain. On the other hand, honest people have fought against this evil. Crores of common men and women have lived lives of integrity. We hear about poor auto-rickshaw drivers returning gold ornaments left in the vehicles to their rightful owners. We hear about taxi drivers who take pains to locate the owners of cell phones left behind. We hear of vegetable vendors who return excess money given by customers.

There comes a time in the history of a country's development when a need is felt for a strong and decisive step. For years, this country has felt that corruption, black money and terrorism are festering sores, holding us back in the race towards development.

Terrorism is a frightening threat. So many have lost their lives because of it. But have you ever thought about how these terrorists get their money? Enemies from across the border run their operations using fake currency notes. This has been going on for years. Many times, those using fake ₹500 and ₹1,000 notes have been caught and many such notes have been seized.

Brothers and sisters,

On the one hand is the problem of terrorism; on the other is the challenge posed by corruption and black money. We began our battle against corruption by setting up an SIT headed by a retired Supreme Court judge, immediately upon taking office. Since then

- a law was passed in 2015 for disclosure of foreign black money;

- agreements with many countries, including the USA, have been made to add provisions for sharing banking information;

- a strict law has come into force from August 2016 to curb benami transactions, which are used to deploy black money earned through corruption and

- a scheme was introduced for declaring black money after paying a stiff penalty.

My dear countrymen,

Through all these efforts, in the last two and a half years, we have brought into the open nearly 1 lakh 25 thousand crore rupees of black money belonging to the corrupt. Honest citizens want this fight against corruption, black money, benami property, terrorism and counterfeiting to continue. Which honest citizen would not be pained by reports of crores worth of currency notes stashed under the beds of government officers? Or by reports of cash found in gunny bags?

The magnitude of cash in circulation is directly linked to the level of corruption. Inflation becomes worse through the deployment of cash earned in corrupt ways. The poor have to bear the brunt of this. It has a direct effect on the purchasing power of the poor and the middle class. You may yourself have experienced when buying land or a house that apart from the amount paid by cheque, a large amount is demanded in cash. This creates problems for an honest person in buying property. The misuse of cash has led to an artificial increase in the cost of goods and services like houses, land, higher education, health care and so on.

High circulation of cash also strengthens the hawala trade which is directly connected to black money and illegal trade in weapons. Debate on the role of black money in elections has been going on for years.

Brothers and sisters,

To break the grip of corruption and black money, we have decided that the ₹500 and ₹1,000 currency notes presently in use will no longer be legal tender from midnight tonight, that is, 8 November 2016. This means that these notes will not be acceptable for transactions from midnight onwards. The ₹500 and ₹1,000 notes hoarded by anti-national and anti-social elements will become just worthless pieces of paper. The rights and the interests of honest, hard-working people will be fully protected. Let me assure you that notes of ₹100, ₹50, ₹20, ₹10, ₹5, ₹2 and ₹1 and all coins will remain legal tender and will not be affected.

This step will strengthen the hands of the common man in the fight against corruption, black money and fake currency. To minimise the difficulties of citizens in the coming days, several steps are being taken.

1. Persons holding old notes of ₹500 or ₹1,000 can deposit these notes in their bank or post office accounts from 10

November until close of banking hours on 30 December 2016 without any limit.

2. Thus, you will have 50 days to deposit your notes and there is no need for panic.

3. Your money will remain yours. You need to have no worry on this point.

4. After depositing your money in your account, you can draw it when you need it.

5. Keeping in mind the supply of new notes, in the first few days, there will be a limit of ₹10,000 per day and ₹20,000 per week. This limit will be increased in the coming days.

6. Apart from depositing your notes in your bank account, another facility will also be there.

7. For your immediate needs, you can go to any bank, head post office or sub post office, show your identity proof such as Aadhaar card, voter card, ration card, passport, PAN card or other approved proofs and exchange your old ₹500 or ₹1,000 notes for new notes.

8. From 10 November until 24 November, the limit for such exchange will be ₹4,000. From 25 November until 30 December, the limit will be increased.

9. There may be some who, for some reason, are not able to deposit their old ₹500 or ₹1,000 notes by 30 December 2016.

10. They can go to specified offices of the Reserve Bank of India up to 31 March 2017 and deposit the notes after submitting a declaration form.

11. On 9 November and in some places on 10 November also, ATMs will not work. In the first few days, there will be a limit of ₹2,000 per day per card.

12. This will be raised to ₹4,000 later.

13. ₹500 and ₹1,000 notes will not be legal tender from midnight. However, for humanitarian reasons, to reduce hardship to citizens, some special arrangements have been made for the first 72 hours, that is until midnight on 11 November.

14. During this period, government hospitals will continue to accept ₹500 and ₹1,000 notes for payment.

15. This is for the benefit of those families whose members may be unwell.

16. Pharmacies in government hospitals will also accept these notes for buying medicines with doctors' prescription.

17. For 72 hours, until midnight on 11 November, railway ticket booking counters, ticket counters of government buses and airline ticket counters at airports will accept the old notes for purchase of tickets. This is for the benefit of those who may be travelling at this time.

18. For 72 hours, ₹500 and ₹1,000 notes will be accepted also at

    • Petrol, diesel and CNG gas stations authorised by public sector oil companies

    • Consumer cooperative stores authorised by state or central government

    • Milk booths authorised by state governments

    • Crematoria and burial grounds

    These outlets will have to keep proper records of stock and collections.

19. Arrangements will be made at international airports for arriving and departing passengers who have ₹500 or

₹1,000 notes of not more than ₹5,000, to exchange them for new notes or other legal tender.

20. Foreign tourists will be able to exchange foreign currency or old notes of not more than ₹5,000 into legal tender.

21. One more thing I would like to mention, I want to stress that in this entire exercise, there is no restriction of any kind on non-cash payments by cheques, demand drafts, debit or credit cards and electronic fund transfer.

Brothers and sisters,

In spite of all these efforts, there may be temporary hardships to be faced by honest citizens. Experience tells us that ordinary citizens are always ready to make sacrifices and face difficulties for the benefit of the nation. I see that spirit when a poor widow gives up her LPG subsidy, when a retired school teacher contributes his pension to the Swachh Bharat mission, when a poor Adivasi mother sells her goats to build a toilet, when a soldier contributes ₹57,000 to make his village clean. I have seen that the ordinary citizen has the determination to do anything, if it will lead to the country's progress.

So, in this fight against corruption, black money, fake notes and terrorism, in this movement for purifying our country, will our people not put up with difficulties for some days? I have full confidence that every citizen will stand up and participate in this *mahayagna*. My dear countrymen, after the festivity of Diwali, now join the nation and extend your hand in this *Imandaari ka Utsav*, this *Pramanikta ka Parv*, this celebration of integrity, this festival of credibility.

I am sure that all political parties, all governments, social services organisations, the media and indeed all sections of the society will take part in this with enthusiasm and make it a success.

My dear countrymen,

Secrecy was essential for this action. It is only now, as I speak to you, that various agencies such as banks, post offices, railways, hospitals and others are being informed. The Reserve Bank, banks and post offices have to make many arrangements at very short notice. Obviously, time will be needed. Therefore, all banks will be closed to the public on 9 November. This may cause some hardship to you. I have full faith that banks and post offices will successfully carry out this great task of national importance. However, I appeal to all of you to help the banks and post offices to meet this challenge with poise and determination.

My dear citizens,

From time to time, based on currency needs, the Reserve Bank with the approval of the central government brings out new notes of higher value. In 2014, the Reserve Bank sent a recommendation for issue of ₹5,000 and ₹10,000 notes. After careful consideration, this was not accepted. Now, as part of this exercise, RBI's recommendation to issue ₹2,000 notes has been accepted. New notes of ₹500 and ₹2,000, with completely new design, will be introduced. Based on past experience, the Reserve Bank will hereafter make arrangements to limit the share of high-denomination notes in the total currency in circulation.

In a country's history, there come moments when every person feels he too should be part of that moment, that he too should make his contribution to the country's progress. Such moments come but rarely. Now, we again have an opportunity where every citizen can join this maha yagna against the ills of corruption, black money and fake notes. The more help you give in this campaign, the more successful it will be.

It has been a matter of concern for all of us that corruption and black money tend to be accepted as part of life. This type of thinking has afflicted our politics, our administration and our society like an infestation of termites. None of our public institutions is free from these termites.

Time and again, I have seen that when the average citizen has to choose between accepting dishonesty and bearing inconvenience, they always choose to put up with inconvenience. They will not support dishonesty.

Once again, let me invite you to make your contribution to this grand sacrifice for cleansing our country, just as you cleaned up your surroundings during Diwali.

Let us ignore the temporary hardship.

Let us join this festival of integrity and credibility.

Let us enable coming generations to live their lives with dignity.

Let us fight corruption and black money.

Let us ensure that the nation's wealth benefits the poor.

Let us enable law-abiding citizens to get their due share.

I am confident in the 125 crore people of India and I am sure country will get success.

Thank you very much. Thanks a lot.

Namaskar.

Bharat Mata Ki Jai.

Demonetisation Episode Shows Why Reserve Bank of India Cannot Be Independent

In the wake of demonetisation, a debate has emerged on independence of RBI. Several former governors of RBI are calling for greater independence of RBI, citing the case of demonetisation as an example of erosion of RBI's independence. We would suggest an opposite line. Demonetisation shows why RBI cannot be fully independent in matters of currency. Suppose RBI decided to demonetise along the lines of what has happened. This would be a case of bunch of unelected officials (babus) to decide on a matter of vital importance for the public without any recourse to the public to punish the decision- makers. In what has happened, the public will have an opportunity to dislodge the decision-makers in next elections if they so wish, which is what democracy is about.

While talking of monetary policy, it is relevant to compare it with defence policy. Issues of defence are, if anything, even more technical than the issues of monetary policy. Yet defence policy is decided by elected civilian authorities with of course full consultation with the defence personnel. In some cases, defence officials may disagree with the decisions of civilian authorities or the other way round. In such cases, the buck stops with the civilian authorities and the technical experts even in such a complex field as defence may either resign or be fired. The same rules should apply to monetary affairs. This of course does not preclude intensive consultations between the civilian authorities and technical experts. If such consultations have been inadequate in the current episode of demonetisation, that is the right issue to discuss. Not who the boss is.

Our obsession with independence of central bank is a colonial hangover where we are trying to copy the Anglo-American world, where the case for such independence was developed in very different circumstances. In our case, the more relevant experience is that of East Asia where monetary policy has been seen as part of the overall economic management of the country with the political leaders in charge with full consultation with technical experts. These are the countries that have shown how to move from a low-income country to a developed country within a generation or so with reasonable price stability. Our Look East/ Act East policy is relevant in this area as in many others. The key theme is that monetary policy is too serious a business to be left to monetary authorities and inflation is too big a job to be left to monetary policy.

On monetary policy as in many other areas, we tend to ape the latest in the West without considering the differences of circumstances. On the issues of independence of RBI, its mandate on controlling inflation, its instrument for controlling inflation, we have been trying to replicate the US/UK strategy and the results have been suboptimal. In this annex, we argue that we have more to learn from our neighbours in East Asia, particularly China, who has achieved an economic transformation similar to what we want.

On the issue of independence of RBI, we suffer from schizophrenia. The de jure position is clear. As per the RBI Act (1934),

> The Central Government may from time to time give such directions to the Bank as it may, after consultation with the Governor of the Bank, consider necessary in the public interest.

However, in an attempt to appear following the fashion in the Western world on independence of the central bank, we pretend that de facto RBI is independent. We thus have the spectacle of minister of finance pleading in public that the governor of RBI should take note of declining inflation and lower the interest rate. This is pathetic. Either the central government should exercise its legal prerogative and ask RBI to lower the interest rate or keep quiet and let RBI do its job.

First, the idea that RBI's professional independence should not be compromised by politicians seeking easy money is disingenuous. Inflation is a serious issue in elections and a political leader is as much interested in controlling inflation as any bureaucrat. In fact, it is the governor of RBI that suffers no consequences for failing in controlling inflation. Thus, giving the governor independent power of controlling inflation is a case of power without responsibility.

Second, following the current fashion, we seem to accept that RBI's primary mandate is to control inflation. This is too narrow a definition of a central bank's job. It should include at least three other objectives: maintaining an appropriate stability in external value of the rupee, promoting growth and employment and maintaining financial stability and probity.

Third, it is absurd to think that RBI can be a lead agent for controlling inflation, particularly in Indian conditions where the price index has a high weightage of agricultural products whose prices are dependent on non-monetary factors and of administered prices and wages outside the jurisdiction of RBI. The pathetic performance of RBI's anti-inflation policy since 2011 is ample enough proof of the limited powers of RBI in controlling inflation.

Fourth, the imported idea that inflation targeting by RBI will influence inflationary expectations is out of touch with reality. In its latest review of monetary policy (April 2015), RBI refers to learned articles from the USA and the UK about the power of central bank's target on inflation in influencing price expectations and the power of price expectations on actual inflation. To quote RBI (2015):

> The experience of inflation targeting countries suggests that a credible monetary policy framework with clarity

about the objective function of the central bank helps in anchoring inflation expectations. In the UK for example, just the announcement of instrument independence for the Bank of England in May 1997 led to an immediate fall in inflation expectations by 50 basis points along the entire term structure (Haldane, 2000). In this context, the Monetary Policy Framework Agreement in India should be able to reinforce the disinflationary forces currently at work and anchor inflation expectations around the medium-term inflation target.

The data on inflationary expectations in India over the last few years published by RBI itself, however, clearly show that these price expectations are not responsive to RBI inflation targets. Nor does actual inflation show much link with inflationary expectations.

In the light of these deplorable experiences on monetary management, there is clearly a need for a new code of conduct and the draft Indian Financial Code (IFC) is a step in the right direction. Unfortunately, the present draft does not pay enough attention to the lessons to be learnt from our own experience or to those of our neighbours such as South Korea, Japan and China who have shown an impressive record on achieving rapid growth with price stability. During the post-war period, 1945–90, when Japan achieved remarkable growth with reasonable price stability, monetary policy was not in a silo but was fully integrated with macro-management policy of the government working through the Ministry of Finance. South Korea which achieved rapid growth during 1962–2000 had an initial period of high inflation until 1980 but an impressive record on price stability with high growth during the subsequent period. For most of this period, the monetary policy worked closely in coordination with fiscal policy and price/wage policy with coordination provided by the Economic Planning Board. Even more impressive is the performance of China in achieving sustained high growth with moderate inflation.

It will be worth our while to study how China handled the issue of monetary policy and what lessons we can learn from that.

China's Law on Monetary Management

China's current law on monetary management was enacted in 1995. It so happens that I was in Beijing at that time as chief of economic unit of the World Bank's Resident Mission in China. The World Bank was not officially engaged in conversation with the government of the issue of monetary management law. But informally, I was often engaged in such conversation. The Western advisers were mostly pushing for independence of the central bank (People's Bank of China [PBOC]), but I was happy to note that the Chinese position was basically that monetary policy is too serious a business to be left to monetary authorities.

The law as it came out is worth studying closely by the Indian authorities, particularly in view of the impressive performance of the Chinese authorities in reconciling price stability with high growth in the period that followed. Some of the provisions of the Chinese law are worth quoting.

> The People's Bank of China shall, under the leadership of the State Council, formulate and implement monetary policies, guard against and eliminate financial risks, and maintain financial stability.

Article 3. 'The aim of monetary policies shall be to maintain the stability of the value of the currency and thereby promote economic growth'.

Article 5. 'The People's Bank of China shall report its decisions to the State Council for approval concerning the annual money supply, interest rate, foreign exchange rates and other important matters specified by the State Council before they are implemented'.

Article 7. 'The People's Bank of China shall, under the leadership of the State Council, implement monetary policies, perform its functions and carry out its business operations independently according to law and be free from intervention by local governments, government departments at various levels, public organizations or individuals'.

It is interesting to note that PBOC is clearly placed under the State Council as an instrument for national economic management.

Draft IFC and Questions Raised in the Light of East Asian Experience

1. **IFC states:** 'The objectives of the Reserve Bank under this Part are to formulate and implement monetary policy'.

Can RBI 'formulate' monetary policy independently of 'fiscal policy' and other supply side policies managed by the government? Shouldn't there be a place in the government that will formulate the overall macro-policies in all their dimensions?

2. **IFC states:** 'The objective of monetary policy is to achieve price stability while striking a balance with the objective of the Central Government to achieve growth'.

Aren't there other objectives such as financial stability which are parts of objectives of monetary policy? What about external value of rupee and financial stability of the economy? Will RBI be the sole judge of whether a right balance is being struck between price stability and growth? Isn't price stability also the objective of the government?

3. IFC states: 'Price stability' means meeting the inflation target.

    a.   '"Inflation" means the year-on-year change expressed in percentage terms in the monthly Consumer Price Index'.

    b.   '"Policy Rate" means a rate at which banks borrow from the Reserve Bank and which is approved by the Monetary Policy Committee as the Policy Rate'.

    c.   'Inflation target for each financial year will be determined in terms of the Consumer Price Index by the Central Government in consultation with the Reserve Bank every three years'.

    d.   'The Reserve Bank must constitute a Monetary Policy Committee to determine by majority vote the Policy Rate required to achieve the inflation target'.

Is consumer price index the only indicator of inflation? What about producer price or asset price? Is policy rate the only instrument for achieving inflation target? Other issues such as money supply, fiscal policy and administered prices are also important. Who will integrate these aspects? As mentioned in the title of this annex, monetary policy can have serious consequences for investment, exports, growth, employment and stability of the economy and it cannot be left to unelected officials. Equally, inflation rate particularly in Indian context is not just a monetary phenomenon. It is very much influenced by fiscal policy, administered prices of food and fuel and public service wages. Monetary policy cannot by itself control inflation, and monetary authorities cannot be held responsible for breaching the inflation targets.

Concluding Remarks

East Asian experience shows clearly that an independent central bank is not necessary to achieve price stability with rapid growth.

In the cases of Japan, South Korea and China, there was no separate silo for monetary policy. Monetary policy, fiscal policy and other issues of macroeconomic management were considered as a package in a central agency which could be Ministry of Finance, or Planning Board or Cabinet.

In the current Indian conditions, it is advisable to learn from East Asian experience and take RBI out of its silo of conservative monetary policy and make it a part of overall development policy-making body in the government. If India is to provide decent employment to its rapidly growing labour force and meet other development priorities such as providing housing, education, health and social security for all in the next 10 years, it will need to achieve double-digit GDP growth. Given the deflationary atmosphere in the world economy, India can achieve such acceleration in growth mainly through internal demand stimulus and without much inflationary pressures as was done by China in the 1980s. However, that would be possible only if there is a central agency co-coordinating different dimensions of macro-management, rather than working in separate silos for monetary, fiscal and supply side-policies.

Agarwala, Ramgopal. *India 2050: A Roadmap to Sustainable Prosperity*. New Delhi: SAGE Publications, 2014.

Ahluwalia, Montek S. 'Demonetisation: The Good, the Bad and the Ugly', *The Mint*, 25 November 2016.

Basu, Kaushik. 'In India, Black Money Makes for Bad Policy', *The New York Times*, 27 November 2016.

————. 'By Way of Preface', *The Indian Express*, 17 March 2017.

Bhagwati, Jagdish. 'War on Black Money', *The Times of India*, 13 December 2016.

Buehn, Andreas, Claudio E. Montenegro, and Friedrich Schneider. 'Shadow Economies All Over the World: New Estimates for 162 Countries from 1999 to 2007'. Policy Research Working Paper 5356, The World Bank Development Research Group Poverty and Inequality Team & Europe and Central Asia Region, Human Development Economics Unit, July 2010.

Chengappa, Raj. 'Newsmaker of the Year', Interview with PM Modi, *India Today*, 9 January 2017.

Chidambaram, P. 'Cashless Economy: A Distracting Mirage', *The Indian Express*, 25 December 2016.

'Contribution of the Unorganised Sector to GDP Report of the Sub Committee of a NCEUS Task Force'. Working Paper 2, June 2008.

'Demonetisation, the Biggest Scam of 2016, Says Chidambaram', *The Economic Times*, 12 February 2017.

Doctor, Vikram. 'The Cycles of Demonetization: A Look Back at Two Similar Experiments in 1946 and 1978', *The Economic Times*, 12 November 2016.

Drew, Elizabeth. *The Corruption of American Politics*. New York: The Overlook Press, 1999.

Economic Survey 2016–17. Ministry of Finance, Government of India, 2017.

Ghosh, Jayati, C.P. Chandrasekhar, and Prabhat Patnaik. *Demonetization Decoded: A Critique of India's Currency Experiment*. Oxford: Routledge, 2017.

Ministry of Finance. *Black Money: White Paper*. New Delhi: Ministry of Finance, Government of India, May 2012.

Gill, S.S. *The Pathology of Corruption*. New Delhi: Harper Collins India, 1998.

Bibliography

Gupta, Anand P. 'Improving the Management of Public Expenditures: Evidence from India'. *The Journal of Governance* 11, (2015, July).

'Issues Paper on Corruption and Economic Growth'. OECD, 2012.

Jain, Sheenu, and Prabhat Pankaj. *Demonetization: What Lies Ahead for Indian Economy?* New Delhi: Bloomsbury, 2017.

Balakrishnan, K.G. 'Judicial Reforms in India', Indo-EU Business Forum, Keynote Address. London, 31 October 2008.

Kapila, Uma, ed. *Demonetisation: The Economists Speak*. New Delhi: Academic Foundation, 2017.

Kashyap, Karan. 'Post Demonetisation: The Investors that are Bullish on India', *Forbes*, 26 January 2017.

Kumar, Arun. *The Black Economy in India*. New Delhi: Penguin Books India, 1999.

Kumar, Rajiv. *Modi and His Challenges*. New Delhi: Bloomsbury, 2016.

Mishra, Pankaj. *Age of Anger: A History of the Present*. London: Allen Lane, 2017.

Pankaj, Prabhat, and Sheenu Jain. *Demonetization: What Lies Ahead for Indian Economy?* New Delhi: Bloomsbury, 2017.

Reddy, C. Rammanohar. *Demonetization and Black Money*. Hyderabad: Orient Blackswan Private Limited, 2017.

Report of the Committee on Prevention of Corruption, Santhanam Committee Report, Ministry of Home Affairs, Government of India, 1962.

Report of the Direct Taxes Enquiry Committee, Wanchoo Committee Report, Ministry of Finance, Government of India, 1971.

Reserve Bank of India. (April 2015). 'Monetary Policy Report'. Available at https://rbi.org.in/Scripts/PublicationsView.aspx?id=16216 (accessed on 17 May 2017).

Rogoff, Kenneth. *The Curse of Cash*. Princeton, NJ: Princeton University Press, 2016.

———. 'India's Cash Bonfire is Too Much. Too Soon', *Financial Times*, 9 December 2016.

Sen, Pronab. 'Shock and Oh Damn', *Ideas for India*, 14 November 2016.

Sengupta, Rajeswari, and Anjali Sharma. 'What does the Currency Ban Mean for Banks?' *The Mint*, 1 December 2016.

Shah, Ajay. 'How to Make Digital Payments Work', *Business Standard*, 27 November 2016.

Singh, Manmohan. 'Making of Mammoth Tragedy', *The Hindu*, 9 December 2016.

Singh, Prakash. 'Police Reforms: Rejuvenate and Transform the Police', *Business Today*, 17 January 2017.

Srivastava, C.P. *Corruption: India's Enemy Within*. New Delhi: Macmillan India Ltd, 2001.

UN (United Nations). *E-Government Survey 2012: E-Government for the People*. Department of Economic and Social Affairs, UN, 2012.

Van Biezen, Ingrid. *Financing Political Parties and Election Campaigns—Guidelines*, Integrated project 'Making Democratic Institutions Work'. Council of Europe, December 2003.

Venugopal, Vasudha. 'Demonetisation in a Booming Economy is Like Shooting at the Tyres of a Racing Car: Jean Dreze', *The Economic Times*, 22 November 2016.

Vittal, N. *Corruption in India: The Roadblock to National Prosperity*. New Delhi: Academic Foundation, 2003.

Index

village romanticism, overcome,
        141–43
vision 2050, 126–28
Wall Street, financial sector from,
        138–39
Indian Civil Services (ICS), 109–10
Indian economy, 2, 3, 23, 37, 39, 51, 105
informal financial sector, 46
informal sector, 3, 37, 45–46, 69, 78–79
information and communication
        technology (ICT), 64, 96–97
    digital monitoring system, 97,
        99–100
    digital payment system, 97–99
international e-government
        development index, 96, 97

Mahatma Gandhi National Rural
        Employment Guarantee Act
        (MGNREGA), 42, 45
MobiKwik, 77
money, quantity theory, 73–74
monumental mismanagement, 35,
        154–55
Moscow Consensus, 7

National Institute of Public Finance
        and Policy (NIPFP), 15–16
net interest income (NII), 47, 48
non-performing assets (NPAs), 47,
        49–51
neo-swadeshi, 146–48

Organisation for Economic
        Co-operation and
        Development (OECD)
        countries, 24
organised loot, 44–45, 87, 103

political finance, reform of, 113–16
    Election Grants Commission,
        119–21
    European Guidelines, 117–19
    money culture, 115

Post Demonetization, 70
Poverty eradication, 129
Pradhan Mantri Garib Kalyan scheme,
        63
    The Prevention of Corruption Act
        (1988), 5
private sector, 7, 13, 95, 139, 144, 145
pseudo-scientific efforts, black money,
        14–15
    National Institute of Public Finance
        and Policy, 15–16
    non-salary income, 15
    shadow economy, 16–18
    World Bank, 16, 18
public sector banks (PSBs), 47, 50, 51

quantity theory of money, 73–74

real estate sector, 70–72, 162
remonetisation, 161
Reserve Bank of India (RBI), 22, 107,
        151–52
    ability, damage of, 32–35
    autonomy of, 152
    hard-earned autonomy, damage of,
        29–32
    professional reputation, damage of,
        32–35
Reserve Bank of India Act (1934),
        28, 29
Right to Education Act (RTE Act), 133
    The Right to Information Act
        (2005), 5–6
RuPay cards, 98

tax collection, 103–4
tax officials, tyranny of, 54–55
terrorism, 81–82
Thatcher–Reagan revolution, 13
transaction costs, 157–58

Wall Street, 138–39
Wanchoo Committee, 19
World Bank, 16–18, 20

Dr Ramgopal Agarwala is Chairman of Pahle India Foundation, New Delhi.

Dr Agarwala graduated from Presidency College, University of Calcutta, and was a gold medalist in MA Economics. He did his PhD in Econometrics from Manchester University. His thesis was later published in the form of a book *An Econometric Model of India* that became a staple read in Indian universities. He joined the World Bank in 1971 and worked at various senior positions across several countries in Asia and Africa, including Bangladesh, Kenya, Botswana, the Philippines, Thailand, South Korea and China. He retired from the World Bank after serving as the Chief of the Economic Unit of the World Bank Resident Mission in Beijing. On his return to India, he began working as a consultant for Asian Development Bank, the World Bank and the UN. He was a Distinguished Fellow at the Research and Information System for Developing Countries, New Delhi, a think tank under the Ministry of External Affairs, Government of India. The most note-worthy among Dr Agarwala's recent publications are *India 2050: A Roadmap for Sustainable Prosperity (2014)* and *The Resurgent India: Ideas and Priorities*, a book co-written with Rajiv Kumar and Rajesh Shah and published in 2015.

About the Author